THE BUDGET FRIENDLY PCOS DIET COOKBOOK FOR BEGINNERS

Easy Pcos diet for meal prep, weight lose, happy hormones, and to boost fertility.

Betty W. Middendorf

Table Of Contents

INTRODUCTION
WHAT IS PCOS?
PCOS CAUSES AND SYMPTOMS
PCOS TREATMENT TRADITIONAL
Understanding the Link Between Diet and PCOS
Foods to Include in Your PCOS Diet
Foods to Avoid or Limit
PCOS- budget Friendly Meal Plan
Calorie and Macronutrient Needs
Portion Control and Balanced Meals
Budget-Friendly Shopping list and Strategies
Benefits of Meal Prep and Batch Cooking
Getting Started with Batch Cooking and Meal Prep
Meal Prepping Tips for Success
Benefits of exercising for PCOS women
Stress Management Strategies for PCOS
The Best and Worst PCOS Exercises

Breakfast

Oatmeal With Berries And Nuts.
Sausage McMuffin
Spicy Chicken Breakfast Bake
Pumpkin Pancakes
TEX-MEX Breakfast Skillet
Granola Bake
Breakfast Blues Porridge
Tomato and Watermelon Salad
Smoothie with protein powder
Greek yogurt with fruit and granola
Whole-wheat toast with avocado
Hard-boiled eggs

Yogurt parfait
Overnight oats
Egg muffins
Breakfast burrito
Breakfast Sandwich

Lunch

Salad With Grilled Chicken or Fish
Soup
Carrot, Orange and Avocado Salad
Panzanella Salad
Sandwich on whole-wheat bread with lean protein and vegetables
Tuna salad sandwich
Chicken Salad Sandwich
Quinoa bowl with black beans, corn, and salsa
Tofu stir-fry
Veggie wrap
Salad with chickpeas
Swiss Chard Quiche
Asian Chicken Slaw
Sweet Potato Noodle Salad

Dinner

Pulled Pork
Creamy Tomato Baked Fish
Zambreros Burrito Bowl
Harvest Chicken Chili
Shrimp Fried Rice
Zuppa Toscana
Slow Cooked Beef and Broccoli

Dessert

Chocolate Mud Cake
Banana Bread

Berry Delight
Ginger Cookies
Chai Tea Frozen Yogurt
Spiced Nut Muffins
Chocolate Chia Pudding
Slow-Cooked Brownies

Snacks
Trail Mix
Guacamole
Zucchini Chips

SMOOTHIES
SUPERCHARGED GREEN SMOOTHIE
NUTTY CHAI SMOOTHIE
SPICY VEGGIE SMOOTHIE
21 DAY MEAL PLAN

INTRODUCTION

As I was 16-year-old, I received a PCOS diagnosis. I had been experiencing irregular periods and weight gain for a few years, but my doctor had always told me that it was just a normal part of puberty. However, when I went to see her for a different issue, she ordered some blood tests and an ultrasound. The results showed that I had PCOS, which is a hormonal disorder that can cause a variety of symptoms, including irregular periods, infertility, weight gain, and excess hair growth.

The news of my diagnosis broke me. Around me, it seemed as if my world was collapsing. I was worried about my fertility, my weight, and my overall health. I was clueless as to what to do or who to contact.

I started researching PCOS and found out that there was a lot of information available. I learned that there is no cure for PCOS, but there are treatments that can help manage the symptoms. I also learned that many women live with PCOS and have successful careers, families, and lives.

I decided to take control of my health and start managing my PCOS. I made some changes to my diet and exercise routine, and I started taking medication. I also started seeing a therapist to help me cope with the emotional impact of my diagnosis.

It's been a few years since I was diagnosed with PCOS, and I'm doing much better. I've lost weight, my periods are regular, and my hair growth is under control.

I decided to write a cookbook to help other women with PCOS. I wanted to share the recipes that have helped me manage my symptoms and improve my overall health and support women who are struggling with PCOS to feel less alone and more empowered

This cookbook includes over 100 recipes that are low in sugar, processed foods, and unhealthy fats. The recipes are also high in fiber, protein, and healthy fats, which are all important for women with PCOS.

If you have PCOS, I encourage you to learn as much as you can about the condition. There is a lot of information available, and it can be very helpful to know what you're dealing with. The choices for treatment should be discussed with your doctor as well. There is no one-size-fits-all treatment for PCOS, so it's important to find what works best for you.

Remember, you are not alone. Many women live with PCOS and have successful careers, families, and lives. You can do this!

WHAT IS PCOS?

A hormonal disorder called PCOS (Polycystic Ovarian Syndrome) may afflict women of all races and ethnicities at any age after puberty and may also result in metabolic issues. If you are obese or have a mother, sister, or aunt who has PCOS, your chance of developing the condition may be increased. It affects roughly 10% of American women of reproductive age and is the main reason for infertility, according to the American Society for Reproductive Medicine.

The following are the three key characteristics of PCOS:
- Increased testosterone levels
- Abnormalities in ovulation
- Ovaries with polycystic

Women who have too much testosterone and often not enough estrogen frequently have irregular ovulation. Every month, when the eggs aren't adequately discharged, cysts start to grow as they gather around the ovaries.

PCOS CAUSES AND SYMPTOMS

PCOS, unfortunately, has a wide range of unknown causes, however, it seems to run in families. PCOS is also associated with obesity and high insulin levels. Since most PCOS patients have insulin resistance, their bodies must manufacture extra insulin to make up for this.

A woman often experiences the following indications and symptoms starting in her late teens or early 20s:

- Irregular cycles missed periods, or very light or heavy cycles
- Having trouble getting pregnant because of erratic ovulation
- Excessive hair growth (hirsutism)
- Increased appetite

- Gaining weight
- On the scalp, hair thinning or falling off
- Acne or oily skin
- Sleep apnea
- Skin darkening, mainly in the crotch, beneath breasts, and along neck creases.
- Skin tags in the neck region or under the arms.

PCOS TREATMENT TRADITIONAL

Although there is no cure, managing symptoms, controlling hormones, and changing one's lifestyle are the main objectives of therapy. In specific circumstances, surgery may be required.

Lifestyle adjustments: If you're overweight, diet and exercise may help you lose weight and keep it off.

Hormone regulation: If you're attempting to become pregnant, your doctor could prescribe drugs that encourage regular ovulation. If you are not attempting to get pregnant, birth control may be advised to manage hormones. Additionally, medication such as metformin may be utilized to aid with blood sugar management.

Treatment of symptoms: If you have excessive hair growth, your doctor may recommend a medication like spironolactone.

Surgery: Laparoscopic ovarian drilling (LOD), a surgical technique, maybe a possibility if fertility drugs are ineffective.

RISKS TO HEALTH FROM PCOS

In addition to making women more likely to develop facial hair and acne, high levels of testosterone also raise their chance of developing illnesses including type 2 diabetes, high blood pressure, and high cholesterol. Each of these conditions has the potential to develop into more serious illnesses like heart disease and stroke later in life.

Infertility, miscarriages, gestational diabetes, endometrial cancer, depression, and anxiety are all conditions that may be brought on by hormonal abnormalities.

PCOS affects the whole body, including how insulin is metabolized, the gut flora, and other metabolic processes including inflammation, albeit each instance is different. Understanding how to balance your hormone levels can help you feel your best, better manage symptoms, and resolve infertility problems.

Lifestyle and dietary factors to consider

Adopting a balanced lifestyle and nutritional strategy may be quite helpful for PCOS women in controlling symptoms and enhancing overall well-being. It is advised to have a well-balanced diet full of entire foods, such as fruits, vegetables, lean meats, and complex carbs. Reducing refined sugars and carbs, boosting fiber consumption, and emphasizing foods with a low glycemic index are some examples of specific dietary approaches. Insulin resistance and PCOS symptoms may both benefit from consistent exercise and weight control.

Understanding the Link Between Diet and PCOS

Diet plays a significant role in managing PCOS because it can help regulate insulin levels, control weight, reduce inflammation, and balance hormones. Women with PCOS often have insulin resistance, which means their bodies have difficulty using insulin effectively. This leads to elevated insulin levels and increased androgen production, contributing to the symptoms of PCOS. By adopting a diet that focuses on controlling blood sugar levels and reducing insulin resistance, women with PCOS can potentially alleviate symptoms and improve their overall health.

Key Dietary Recommendations for Managing PCOS

Emphasize Whole Unprocessed Foods: Incorporate a variety of nutrient-dense foods into your diet, including fruits, vegetables, whole grains, lean proteins, and healthy fats. These foods provide essential vitamins, minerals, and fiber while promoting satiety and stable blood sugar levels.

Opt for Low-Glycemic Index (GI) Foods: Choose carbohydrates with a low glycemic index, such as whole grains, legumes, and non-starchy vegetables. Low-GI foods are digested more slowly, resulting in a gradual release of glucose into the bloodstream and preventing spikes in insulin levels.

Prioritize Lean Proteins: Include lean protein sources such as poultry, fish, tofu, tempeh, and legumes in your meals. Protein helps stabilize blood sugar levels, promotes satiety, and supports muscle maintenance.

Healthy Fats: Avocados, almonds, seeds, and olive oil are examples of sources of healthful fats. These fats provide essential fatty acids and help regulate hormone production.

Reduce Added Sugars and Refined Carbohydrates: Minimize your consumption of sugary beverages, processed foods, sweets, and refined grains. These foods can lead to rapid spikes in blood sugar and insulin levels, exacerbating PCOS symptoms.

Balance Macronutrients: Aim for a balanced distribution of macronutrients, including carbohydrates, proteins, and fats. Balancing your meals can help promote stable blood sugar levels and manage insulin resistance.

Portion Control and Mindful Eating: Practice portion control to avoid overeating and focus on mindful eating. Take your time, enjoy your food, and pay attention to your body's hunger and fullness signs.

Drink enough water all day long to maintain your hydration and general wellness.

Foods to Include in Your PCOS Diet

High-Fiber Foods: Fiber-rich foods help regulate blood sugar levels, promote healthy digestion, and support weight management. Include whole grains like quinoa, brown rice, and oats in your diet. Add an array of colorful vegetables such as broccoli, spinach, kale, and Brussels sprouts. Legumes like lentils, chickpeas, and black beans are also excellent sources of fiber and plant-based protein.

Lean Proteins: Incorporating lean proteins in your PCOS diet helps stabilize blood sugar levels and supports muscle health. Choose options such as skinless poultry, fish (like salmon and trout), tofu, tempeh, and Greek yogurt. Plant-based proteins like lentils, quinoa, and edamame are also great alternatives.

Healthy Fats: Including healthy fats in your diet supports hormone production, aids in nutrient absorption, and provides a feeling of satiety. Opt for foods like avocados, nuts (such as almonds, walnuts, and pistachios), seeds (like flaxseeds and chia seeds), and olive oil. These fats also contain omega-3 fatty acids, which have anti-inflammatory properties.

Antioxidant-Rich Fruits: Colorful fruits are packed with antioxidants that help reduce inflammation and combat oxidative stress. Berries, such as blueberries, strawberries, and raspberries, are particularly beneficial due to their high fiber and low sugar content. Other antioxidant-rich fruits include citrus fruits, pomegranates, and cherries.

Calcium-Rich Foods: Calcium plays a vital role in maintaining bone health and hormone balance. Choose calcium-rich options like low-fat dairy products (if tolerated), fortified plant-based milk alternatives, tofu (made with calcium sulfate), and leafy green vegetables such as kale, collard greens, and bok choy.

Vitamin D Sources: Vitamin D deficiency is common among individuals with PCOS and can impact hormone regulation. Include foods fortified with vitamin D, such as fortified plant-based milk, cereals, and mushrooms. Spend time outside to enable your body to produce vitamin D naturally from sunshine.

Foods Rich in Magnesium: Magnesium is important for insulin sensitivity and plays a role in managing PCOS symptoms. Incorporate magnesium-rich foods like leafy green vegetables, whole grains, legumes, nuts, and seeds into your diet.

Herbal Teas: Certain herbal teas can support hormone balance and provide relaxation. Spearmint tea has shown potential benefits in reducing androgen levels, while chamomile tea can help reduce stress and promote better sleep.

Water and Hydration:
Proper hydration is crucial for overall health and hormone regulation. Limit sugary drinks and drink enough water throughout the day.

Foods to Avoid or Limit

Processed and sugary foods should be limited or avoided, including fast food, packaged snacks, sugary beverages, and desserts. These meals often include high concentrations of harmful fats, added sugars, and processed carbs, which may cause blood sugar abnormalities and weight gain. Every time you can, choose entire, unadulterated meals.

Refined Carbohydrates: Foods manufactured from refined grains, such as white bread, white rice, and pasta, have a high glycemic index and send blood sugar levels skyrocketing quickly. Hormonal abnormalities and insulin resistance may result from this. Instead, choose whole grains that are higher in fiber and minerals, such as quinoa, brown rice, and whole wheat bread.

Foods heavy in saturated fats, such as fatty meat cuts, whole-fat dairy products, and fried foods, may promote inflammation and lead to insulin resistance. Limiting your consumption of these items may help you control PCOS symptoms. Select lean protein sources, dairy products with less fat, or dairy substitutes, and healthier cooking techniques like baking, grilling, or steaming.

Trans Fats: These synthetic fats are included in several processed foods, margarine, and baked products. They may heighten the risk of heart disease, exacerbate insulin resistance, and enhance inflammation. Avoid foods that contain trans fats or partially hydrogenated oils by reading food labels.

Foods having a high glycemic index, such as refined grains, white potatoes, and sweetened drinks, induce a sharp spike in blood sugar levels. This may impair insulin sensitivity and result in weight gain. To encourage stable blood sugar levels, choose foods with low glycemic index such as whole fruits, quinoa, and sweet potatoes.

Alcohol and excessive caffeine use: While moderate caffeine use may not have a major effect on PCOS, excessive caffeine use may disturb hormone balance and increase insulin resistance. Similar to how excessive alcohol use may impair liver function and exacerbate insulin resistance. It's recommended to avoid alcohol completely and restrict your intake of caffeinated drinks.

Dairy Products (if Intolerant): Some PCOS sufferers may have a sensitivity to or lactose intolerance to dairy products. Consider switching to lactose-free or plant-based substitutes like almond milk, soy milk, or coconut yogurt if you encounter symptoms such as gastrointestinal problems or other after-dairy symptoms.

PCOS- budget Friendly Meal Plan

Embrace Whole Foods: Whole foods are not only economical but also nutrient-dense. They consist of fresh produce, nutritious grains, legumes, and inexpensive protein sources including eggs, tofu, and beans. These foods are bursting with vital nutrients, fiber, and antioxidants that may help control PCOS symptoms. For affordable and healthful choices, center your meals around these healthy foods.

Shop locally and seasonally whenever possible since the product is often cheaper and fresher. To get fresh, inexpensive fruits and veggies, go to your neighborhood farmers' markets or sign up for CSA programs. When a certain food item is out of season, frozen fruits and vegetables are a practical and affordable replacement.

Plan Meals in advance: Meal planning is a vital tactic for time and money saving. Spend some time each week planning your meals, taking into account your finances and PCOS nutritional needs. Make a list of the items you'll need and plan your shopping appropriately. This will save you from making impulsive purchases and guarantee you have everything you need to make your meals.

Cook in Bulk and Freeze: Cooking food in bulk and freezing it is a great method to save time and money. Soups, stews, casseroles, and other PCOS-friendly foods should be prepared in bigger amounts and divided into individual portions. These servings may be frozen for later meals, giving you quick-to-prepare healthy alternatives.

Utilize budget-friendly Protein Sources: Protein is a crucial part of a PCOS-friendly diet. Choose affordable protein options including eggs, canned beans, lentils, and tofu. These choices are friendly on your money while offering a lot of protein. For a well-rounded meal, add them to salads, stir-fries, and grain bowls.

Choose plant-based proteins: These include beans, lentils, and chickpeas, which are not only inexpensive but also high in fiber and minerals. They may serve as the basis for meals that are both affordable and filling. To add variety and flavor to your meal plan, experiment with ideas for lentil soups, bean-based salads, and vegetarian chili.

Minimize Processed food: your intake of processed foods as much as possible since they are often pricey and have poor nutritional value. They may also make PCOS symptoms worse. Limit your consumption of convenience meals, fizzy beverages, and packaged snacks. Instead, concentrate on eating whole, unprocessed foods since they are more cheap and good for your health.

Calorie and Macronutrient Needs

Calorie requirements:
Calorie requirements vary from person to person and rely on things like age, weight, height, exercise level, and metabolic rate. To get a healthy weight, it's essential to maintain a balance between energy intake and expenditure. While weight reduction, if necessary, might improve hormonal balance and general health, it can also make PCOS symptoms worse.

Macronutrients and PCOS:
Our food is made up of three different types of nutrients: carbs, proteins, and lipids. In managing PCOS, each macronutrient has a special function.

Carbohydrates:
Choose complex carbs that are high in fiber, such as whole grains, legumes, and veggies. These support stable blood sugar levels and aid in controlling insulin resistance, a prevalent issue in PCOS. Limit processed meals and refined sugars, and strive for a balanced daily intake of carbs.

Proteins: Proteins are essential for maintaining hormone synthesis, metabolism, and muscular health. Include lean protein sources such as chicken, fish, tofu, lentils, and dairy (if permitted). To support your general health and PCOS treatment objectives, aim for a moderate intake of protein.

Focus on ingesting healthy fats, such as those in avocados, nuts, seeds, olive oil, and fatty fish. These facilitate the generation of hormones and offer vital fatty acids. Limit saturated and trans fats, which are often present in processed and fried meals and may cause inflammation and insulin resistance.

Portion Control and Balanced Meals

Portion management is the practice of regulating how much food you eat in order to balance nutrient intake with moderation. This routine promotes hormonal balance and optimal weight maintenance. To avoid insulin spikes, maintain consistent blood sugar levels, and control symptoms associated with weight gain in PCOS, portion control is very crucial.

Creating Balanced Meals: Creating balanced meals is crucial for fueling your body and giving it the nutrients it needs. The essential elements that should be included in your balanced meals for people with PCOS are broken down as follows:

Lean Proteins: Include lean protein-rich foods including skinless chicken, fish, tofu, lentils, and low-fat dairy. These protein-rich meals help with hormone synthesis, muscular function, and satiety.

Complex carbs: Opt for complex carbs that are high in fiber, such as whole grains, quinoa, brown rice, and legumes. These slow-digesting carbohydrates provide steady blood sugar levels and assist in controlling insulin resistance.

Include sources of healthful fats including avocados, nuts, seeds, olive oil, and fatty seafood. These fats assist hormone production, the absorption of fat-soluble vitamins, and the provision of vital fatty acids.

Fill your dish with a mix of bright fruits and veggies. These nutrient-dense foods are brimming with vitamins, minerals, and antioxidants that promote general health and PCOS control.

Practice Mindful Eating: In addition to portion management and balanced meals, practicing mindful eating may have a good effect on your relationship with food and assist in managing the symptoms of PCOS. By eating deliberately and appreciating each mouthful, one may practice mindful eating. You may more easily determine when you are full and prevent overeating by concentrating on the eating experience.

Planning and preparing meals in advance may help to ensure that portions are controlled and that meals are balanced. Consider your dietary requirements and preferences when you plan your meals in advance. You have control over the quantity and quality of the ingredients utilized when you prepare meals at home. To make sure you have wholesome meals prepared to eat during the week, think about bulk cooking and meal planning.

Budget-Friendly Shopping list and Strategies

COMPLEX CARBOHYDRATES
- Oat
- Starchy Root Vegetables

(potatoes, sweet potatoes, cassava and carrot)
- Brown Rice
- Whole wheat Pasta
- Legumes

(beans, black eyed peas, chickpea, & lentils)
- Bread and tortilla

VEGETABLES
- Frozen Broccoli
- Cucumber
- Frozen Stir Fry Veggies
- Frozen corn
- Cabbage
- Onions
- Lettuce

- Garlic
- Spinach
- Kale
- Frozen cauliflower
- Celery
- Canned tomatoes and tomato sauce

FRUITS
- Bananas
- Cantaloupe
- Watermelon in summertime
- Apples
- Pears
- Oranges
- Frozen berries

LOW-FAT OR FAT-FREE DAIRY
- Cheese

(whole cheddar and mozzarella)
- Yogurt (Plain Greek)
- Milk

(or plant-based such as unsweetened coconut milk)

HEALTHY FATS
- Olive oil
- Peanuts
- Peanut butter
- Avocado
- Pumpkin &
- Sunflower Seeds

LEAN PROTEIN
- Eggs
- Whole chicken

(Chicken thighs, Chicken breasts)
- Ground meat (85% lean)
- Beef
  (skirt steak, Chuck roast)
- Sausages (Ground turkey or chicken)
- Plant-based protein
- Canned fish
- White-flesh fish

Plan Ahead and Make a Shopping List: A cost-effective approach that guarantees you only purchase what you need is to plan your meals in advance and make a shopping list. Make a list of the items you'll need and plan your meals for the next week before you go shopping. By doing this, you may stay away from impulsive purchases and concentrate on making healthy food selections that will aid in managing your PCOS.

Shop Locally and Seasonally: By choosing seasonal products, you may support regional farmers while also saving money. Fruits and vegetables that are in season are often more plentiful and less expensive. To get fresh, inexpensive food, check out your neighborhood farmers' markets or consider community-supported agriculture (CSA) initiatives. If you have room for a tiny garden or simply a few potted plants, you may also think about producing your own herbs and veggies.

Accept Whole Foods: Stocking your basket with whole foods is good for your health and your wallet. Whole foods including whole grains, legumes, fruits, and vegetables are often less expensive than processed and packaged meals. These nutrient-dense choices include necessary vitamins, minerals, and fiber that promote hormone balance and general well-being.

Compare prices and look for discounts: To get the greatest prices on PCOS-friendly meals, take advantage of shop flyers, online sales, and coupons. When it makes financial sense, compare costs at other retailers and think about purchasing in bulk. Your long-term shopping costs will be reduced if you buy non-perishable goods like grains, beans, and spices in bigger amounts and at a cheaper cost.

Use Frozen and Canned Foods: Frozen fruits and veggies, as well as canned foods like beans and tomatoes, may be helpful partners in your cost-effective PCOS shopping. These products often cost less money, last longer, and keep their nutritious content. They make it simple and fast to prepare meals, ensuring you always have wholesome alternatives on hand.

Reduce Food Waste: This practice is both economical and ecologically good. Plan your meals to make the most of the foods you have on hand, and find inventive ways to use up leftovers. Make homemade vegetable broth from vegetable waste, and freeze any leftovers for later use. You can stretch your budget further if you are aware of food waste.

Purchase in large quantities and store properly:
Bulk purchases of certain pantry essentials, including grains, nuts, and seeds, may be more cost-effective. For access to reasonably priced bulk products, look for bulk bins at grocery shops or think about joining a neighborhood co-op. Just be sure to store them carefully in sealed containers to preserve freshness and avoid spoiling.

When buying packaged goods, take care to read labels. Look for inexpensive choices that suit your PCOS dietary requirements, such as low-sugar, whole-grain, and minimally processed goods. Focus on using basic, healthful products rather than pricey goods with extraneous additives.

Benefits of Meal Prep and Batch Cooking

Time and Effort Savings: By cooking larger quantities of food at once, you can minimize daily cooking time, freeing up valuable time for other activities.

Budget-Friendly Approach: Planning and preparing meals in advance can help you make the most of your ingredients, reduce food waste, and avoid impulse purchases.

Nutritional Control: With batch cooking, you have control over the ingredients used, allowing you to prioritize nutrient-dense foods that support PCOS management.

Portion Control: Preparing meals in advance allows you to portion out meals based on your nutritional needs, supporting balanced eating and preventing overeating.

Convenient and Stress-Free: Having pre-prepared meals on hand reduces the need for last-minute cooking decisions and helps you avoid unhealthy takeaway options.

Getting Started with Batch Cooking and Meal Prep

Create a Weekly Meal Plan: Begin by creating a weekly meal plan. Consider incorporating a balance of proteins, whole grains, healthy fats, and plenty of vegetables to support your PCOS diet.

Make a Shopping List: Once your meals are planned, create a detailed shopping list to ensure you have all the necessary ingredients on hand.

Choose Batch-Friendly Recipes: Look for recipes that can easily be scaled up and that will hold well when refrigerated or frozen. Soups, stews, casseroles, and grain-based salads are great options for batch cooking.
Cook in Bulk: Dedicate a few hours during the week or on the weekend to cook larger quantities of food. Prepare multiple servings of proteins, grains, and roasted or steamed vegetables.

Portion and Store: Divide the cooked food into individual or family-sized portions and store them in airtight containers or freezer-safe bags. Label them with the date and contents for easy identification.

Freeze for Future Use: If you're batch cooking for longer-term storage, consider freezing some portions for future weeks. This way, you can rotate meals and enjoy a variety of flavors throughout the month.

Streamline Prep Time: To save time during meal prep, wash and chop vegetables in advance, and pre-cook grains or legumes to have them ready to use in different dishes.

Meal Prepping Tips for Success

Invest in Quality Containers: Use sturdy, reusable containers that are microwave and dishwasher-safe for easy reheating and cleaning.
Rotate and Reuse: Plan your meals in a way that allows you to rotate leftovers throughout the week, preventing monotony. Repurpose cooked ingredients into different dishes to keep meals interesting.
Take Advantage of Simplicity: Focus on recipes that use common ingredients and simple cooking techniques to minimize cost and preparation time.
Use Seasonal and Budget-Friendly Ingredients: Incorporate seasonal produce and affordable pantry staples to keep costs down while enjoying fresh and flavorful meals.

Don't Forget Snacks: Prepare healthy snacks in advance, such as pre-portioned nuts, chopped fruits, or homemade energy balls, to satisfy cravings and avoid reaching for processed snacks.

Physical Exercise and PCOS

The management of PCOS requires regular exercise. It may aid in weight loss, increased fertility, and improved insulin sensitivity. Exercise may also aid in the reduction of symptoms including mood swings, hirsutism, and acne.

Women with PCOS should engage in at least 150 minutes of moderate-intensity aerobic exercise each week, according to the American College of Obstetricians and Gynecologists (ACOG).

Women with PCOS should do strength-training activities two or more times per week in addition to aerobic activity, according to ACOG. Exercises that focus on building muscle and strengthening bones are known as strength-training exercises.

If you've never exercised before, it's important to start off slowly and gradually increase the duration and intensity of your workouts.

The management of PCOS requires regular exercise. It may assist in enhancing your general health and well-being and lowering your chance of suffering from significant health issues.

Benefits of exercising for PCOS women

*Improves insulin sensitivity: Insulin is a hormone that aids in the body's usage of glucose as fuel. Insulin resistance, which occurs when cells do not react appropriately to insulin, is common in PCOS-afflicted women. This may result in excessive blood sugar levels and an elevated risk of type 2 diabetes. Exercise may assist to increase insulin sensitivity, which can help to decrease blood sugar levels and minimize the risk of type 2 diabetes.

* **Decreases body weight:** Women with PCOS often struggle with being overweight. Gaining weight may exacerbate insulin resistance and make it more difficult to control other PCOS symptoms. Exercise may aid in weight loss, which can assist to improve insulin sensitivity and other PCOS symptoms.

* **Enhances fertility:** Women with PCOS often struggle to conceive. By enhancing ovulation and egg quality, exercise may help enhance fertility in PCOS-afflicted women.

* **Relieves acne, hirsutism, and mood swing symptoms:** PCOS may result in a number of symptoms, including acne, hirsutism (excessive hair growth), and mood swings. By lowering inflammation and increasing insulin sensitivity, exercise may help to alleviate these symptoms.

Exercise provides several advantages for general health and well-being, including lowering the risk of heart disease, stroke, type 2 diabetes, and certain forms of cancer. Mood, sleep, and energy levels may all be improved by exercise.

How to create an Exercise Routine for PCOS

1. Consult with your physician. It's crucial to consult your doctor before beginning any new workout program. They can assist you in developing a personalized workout program that is both safe and efficient.

2. Begin slowly and gradually increase the length and intensity of your exercises. If you've never exercised before, it's important to start off slowly and gradually increase the duration and intensity of your workouts. This

can help you avoid injuries and make sure that you can maintain your workout regimen.

3. Select an enjoyable pastime. You're less likely to persist with your exercises if you don't love them. Choose an activity that you love and that fits into your lifestyle from the many various sorts that are available.

4. Establish realistic goals. Be careful not to try to do too much too quickly. As you grow fitter, progressively increase the length and intensity of your exercises from short, simple ones.

5. Find an exercise buddy. You may maintain motivation and accountability by exercising with a companion.

6. Include physical activity in your daily routine. Just as you would with any other essential appointment, allocate time in your day for exercise.

7. Don't be reluctant to seek assistance. Speak to your doctor or a professional personal trainer if you need assistance selecting an exercise program or learning how to adapt activities to your particular requirements.

Stress Management Strategies for PCOS

Stress may exacerbate PCOS symptoms and make it more challenging to manage the illness. Several stress-reduction methods may assist women with PCOS decrease stress and enhance their general health and well-being:

Exercise: Exercise is a fantastic strategy to lower stress levels and enhance insulin sensitivity. Try to get 30 minutes or more of moderate exercise into your schedule on most days of the week.

Yoga is a mind-body workout that incorporates physical postures, breathing techniques, and meditation. Yoga may assist to lower stress, increase insulin sensitivity, and elevate mood.

Meditation: A mind-body technique, meditation includes cleansing the mind of all ideas and concentrating on the present moment. Stress reduction, better sleep, and mood enhancement are all benefits of meditation.

Deep breathing is a basic stress-reduction strategy. Take a few deep breaths in through your nose and out of your mouth if you are feeling agitated.

Aromatherapy: Aromatherapy employs essential oils to encourage relaxation and lower tension. Consider putting a few drops of essential oil in a warm bath or diffusing it around your house.

Massage: Receiving a massage may help you feel happier, sleep better, and decrease stress.

Spend time in nature: Spending time in nature may assist to lower stress and boost mood. Take a stroll in the park, relax by the water, or go hiking.

Get adequate sleep: Lack of sleep increases stress levels and makes it harder to control PCOS symptoms.
Attempt to get 7-8 hours of sleep per night.

Eat a nutritious diet: A good diet may help you feel less stressed and have better insulin sensitivity. Steer clear of processed meals, sugary beverages, and excessive quantities of coffee and alcohol.

Talk to someone you can trust: Speaking with a friend, family member, therapist, or another trustworthy individual may help you manage stress and enhance your general well-being

The Best and Worst PCOS Exercises

Training in Strength

Many PCOS symptoms, such as insulin resistance and a sluggish metabolism, may be helped by strength training, which includes using weights or bodyweight-focused exercises. Additionally, strength training promotes the growth of muscle mass, which raises the body's metabolic rate both during exercise and during rest. Remember to provide enough time for your body to recuperate and rebuild muscle tissue in between strength training sessions.

High Intensity Interval Training (HIIT) HIIT exercises

are characterized by brief bursts of physically demanding activity followed by recovery periods of reduced intensity. According to research, women with PCOS who engage in HIIT-style exercises had better hormone management, improved body composition, a lower BMI overall, and better blood glucose control.

These women had a decreased future risk of having metabolic syndrome, according to studies conducted throughout time. The most successful kind of exercise for PCOS-affected women is HIIT. These exercises are quite taxing on the body, however. If you include HIIT exercises into your regimen, be sure you arrange enough time for relaxation and recuperation. According to research, doing HIIT-style exercises for 2-3 days a week is adequate to reap the PCOS-related advantages.

Yoga

Due to its function in stress management, yoga has been recognized for its capacity to assist with PCOS treatment. Since hormone control plays a significant role in PCOS, stress management must be given top priority to prevent the release of stress hormones. Your stress hormone, cortisol, rises along with insulin, which might exacerbate the condition of insulin resistance. According to research, practicing yoga or mindfulness meditation even for only ten minutes, three times a week, can have long-lasting benefits.

Worst

Cardio

Although cardiovascular activity has numerous advantages, it may also work against PCOS control. Running, jumping rope, and cycling are all examples of cardiovascular exercise. Certain hormones, such as androgens and the stress hormone cortisol, may be elevated by excessive exercise. The body reacts to increased amounts of these hormones by producing more insulin, which makes controlling blood sugar levels more challenging. But don't let this stop you from engaging in any cardiac activity. In addition to helping to maintain a healthy weight and enhance cardiovascular function, exercise offers numerous additional advantages. The objective is to balance cardio with other types of exercise and to avoid overdoing it.

Repetition: Every kind of workout has something unique to offer. It's crucial to vary your training program and make sure you're not overworking one particular region if you want the finest outcomes. The ideal workout combines active recuperation, cardio, and strength training.

Skipping recovery days: Concentrate on "active recovery" days rather than rest days. Active recovery refers to continuing to move while giving your body time to recover from exercises of a greater intensity. Schedule recovery days at least 2-3 times each week, just as you would higher intensity training days. A long, stroll, mild yoga, an easy bike ride, or bringing your pet to the dog park to play are all examples of active recuperation.

The activity you consistently do has the most impact on PCOS when it comes to exercising. Choose a choice of enjoyable hobbies that make you feel fantastic! The most beneficial forms of exercise for treating PCOS, according to research, are HIIT and strength training, but what's even more crucial is that you're moving your body in a manner that feels good.

Breakfast

Oatmeal With Berries And Nuts

Prep Time 5 mins Cook Time 5 mins

Ingredients:
- ☐ 1 cup rolled oats
- ☐ 1 cup unsweetened almond milk
- ☐ 1/2 cup berries
  (such as blueberries, raspberries, or strawberries)
- ☐ 1/4 cup chopped nuts
  (such as almonds, walnuts, or pecans)
- ☐ 1 tablespoon honey (optional)

Instructions
- In a small pot, combine the oats and almond milk. Bring to a boil over medium heat, then reduce heat to low and simmer for 5 minutes, or until the oats are cooked through.
- Stir in the berries, nuts, and honey (if using).
- Serve immediately.

Nutrition Per Serve
Calories: 300| Fat: 10g| Fat: 1g|Cholesterol: 0mg |Carbohydrates: 45g Fiber: 5g| Sugar: 15g| Protein: 10g

Sausage McMuffin

Prep Time 10 mins Cook Time 10 mins Serving 1

INGREDIENTS

PROTEIN
- ☐ 4 oz Sausage patties (or swap for beef patty)
- ☐ 1 Egg

PANTRY
- ☐ 2 tbsp Ghee (divided)
- ☐ 1 tbsp Almond milk
- ☐ 1 tbsp Olive oil
- ☐ 1 tbsp Coconut flour
- ☐ 2 tbsp Almond flour
- ☐ 1/2 tsp Baking powder
- ☐ 1/4 tsp Salt

FRUIT
- ☐ 1/2 Avocado (mashed)

INSTRUCTIONS
- Ghee should be melted over medium-high heat. The beef or sausage patties should be cooked and placed aside.
- Egg, almond milk, olive oil, coconut flour, almond flour, baking soda, and salt should all be combined in a small bowl before making the biscuit.
- Two 3.5" round biscuit cutters should be greased in the pan with more ghee.
- Distribute the biscuit mixture equally into each mold after setting the cutters into the pan.
- Reduce the temperature. Cook the biscuit mixture for approximately 4 minutes, or until almost done.
- Flip the biscuits after taking the molds off with care. For approximately one minute, cook.
- Assemble the "McMuffin" by sandwiching a mashed avocado between the two biscuits and the beef patty.

NUTRITION INFORMATION: YIELD: 1 SERVING SIZE: 1
CALORIES: 1068| FAT: 98g|CHOLESTEROL: 349mg|CARBOHYDRATES: 19g|FIBER: 9g|SUGAR: 4g|PROTEIN: 34g

Spicy Chicken Breakfast Bake

PREP TIME: 15 MINUTES COOK TIME: 40 MINUTES Serving 4
INGREDIENTS
PROTEIN
- ☐ 8 Eggs
- ☐ 8 oz Chicken breasts

PANTRY
- ☐ 4 tbsp Almond milk (or full-fat coconut milk)
- ☐ 4 tbsp Mayonnaise
- ☐ 1/3 cup Hot sauce
- ☐ 1 tsp Garlic powder
- ☐ 1 tsp Onion powder
- ☐ 1/2 tsp Paprika
- ☐ 1 tsp Dried dill
- ☐ 1 tsp Salt
- ☐ 4 tbsp Ranch dressing

VEGETABLE
- ☐ 1 Scallion (diced)

INSTRUCTIONS
- Add salt and pepper to taste, then bake, broil, or fry the chicken until fully done. After allowing it cool, chop or shred it into bite-sized pieces.

- Grease a casserole dish that measures 9 x 13" (23 x 33 cm) and preheat the oven to 375°F (190°C).
- In a large bowl, whisk together the eggs, almond milk, mayonnaise, and spicy sauce. Add salt, scallions, paprika, dried dill, garlic powder, onion powder, and cooked chicken by stirring everything together.
- The mixture should be poured into the casserole and baked for 35 to 40 minutes, or until the eggs are fully cooked and the center is set.
- Ranch dressing should be drizzled over the cut before eating.
- Keep chilled for up to four days in a container with a tight closure.

NUTRITION INFORMATION: SERVING SIZE: 1
CALORIES: 410 FAT: 29g CHOLESTEROL: 430mg CARBOHYDRATES: 5gFIBER: 1g SUGAR: 2g PROTEIN: 31g

Pumpkin Pancakes

PREP TIME: 15 MINUTES COOK TIME: 20 MINUTES Serving 4
INGREDIENTS
PROTEIN
- ☐ 4 Eggs

PANTRY
- ☐ 1/2 cup Pumpkin puree
- ☐ 1 tsp Vanilla extract

- ☐ 1 tsp Ground Ceylon cinnamon
- ☐ 1 tsp Pumpkin pie spice
- ☐ 1/2 tsp Baking soda
- ☐ 1/8 tsp Salt
- ☐ 2 tbsp Coconut flour
  (optional, incase your batter is too runny)
- ☐ 1 tbsp Ghee (for the batter)
- ☐ 2 tbsp Ghee (for frying pancakes)
- ☐ 1/2 cup Coconut yogurt

FRUIT
- ☐ 1 cup Frozen berries

INSTRUCTIONS

- The eggs, pumpkin puree, vanilla extract, cinnamon, pie spice, baking soda, and salt should all be combined in a large mixing dish. To make the mixture entirely smooth, whisk and combine. To prevent any lumps with the dry ingredients
- The amount of pumpkin puree and eggs you use will determine how thick or runny the batter is, so you may need to experiment a bit to get the ideal consistency. In general, it is preferable to have a somewhat runnier mixture than you would be used to. However, if the batter needs to be thickened, combine it with 1-2 tablespoons of coconut flour and let it rest for about 10 minutes.
- Heat a sizable skillet to a medium-low temperature. Before putting the pan back on the heat, immediately melt the ghee and stir it into the batter to finish preparing it.
- Pour the pancake batter into the skillet, then add a good quantity of ghee.
- Flip the pancakes over once a few bubbles start to emerge and cook them through on the other side. Till all of the batters are consumed, repeat the procedure.
- Turn down the heat and cook your pancakes more slowly if you discover that they are burned on the exterior but undercooked on the interior. To get them properly, a little practice may be necessary.

- Add some berries and yogurt to the pancakes as a garnish. I often just thaw and stir a few frozen berries in a small saucepan to make a simply mixed berry compote. You may start as soon as they become soft.

Nutrition SERVING SIZE: 1
CALORIES: 468 FAT: 31g CHOLESTEROL: 422mg CARBOHYDRATES: 31g FIBER: 6g SUGAR: 19g PROTEIN: 18g

TEX-MEX Breakfast Skillet

PREP TIME: 15 MINUTES COOK TIME: 20 MINUTES
Servings 4

INGREDIENTS

PROTEIN
- ☐ 1 1/2 lb Ground beef (beef mince)
- ☐ 4 Eggs

PANTRY
- ☐ 1/2 cup Olive oil (divided)
- ☐ 1 cup Salsa
- ☐ 1 tsp Ground cumin
- ☐ 1/2 tsp Chili powder
- ☐ 1 tsp Salt
- ☐ 1/2 tsp Black pepper

VEGETABLE
- ☐ 1 lb Zucchini
  (or yellow squash, sliced into thin half-moons)
- ☐ 1 Onion (diced)
- ☐ 1 Red bell pepper (cut into strips)
- ☐ 1/2 cup Fresh cilantro (minced)
- ☐ 3 Scallions (sliced)

INSTRUCTIONS
- The onion should be fried for approximately 5 minutes, or until tender, in a large pan over medium-high heat.
- A large bowl should be put aside after cooking the squash, bell pepper, cumin, and chili powder for a further 5 minutes, or until the vegetables are just barely soft.
- Re-heat the pan, add additional oil, and cook the beef, breaking it up with a spoon or spatula as you go until it is well browned. Add the meat, veggies, and salt and pepper to the same bowl and stir to fully combine.
- Reduce the heat to low and put the skillet back on the burner with a generous amount of olive oil. Add the eggs to the pan and stir to scramble after whisking them with a little additional salt.
- Add the meat, veggies, and salsa back in after the eggs are nearly set, and stir everything together thoroughly.
- Serve with cilantro and scallions on top.

Nutrition SERVING SIZE: 1
CALORIES: 835 FAT: 62g CHOLESTEROL: 337mg CARBOHYDRATES: 14g FIBER: 4g SUGAR: 7g PROTEIN: 55g

Granola Bake

PREP TIME: 25 MINUTES COOK TIME: 35 MINUTES
Servings 6

INGREDIENTS

PANTRY
- ☐ 2 tbsp Flaxseed/Linseed meal
- ☐ 1/2 cup Almonds
- ☐ 1/2 cup Walnuts
- ☐ 1/2 cup Pecans
- ☐ 1/3 cup Coconut flakes
- ☐ 1 tbsp Coconut oil (melted, for toasting nuts)
- ☐ 1/2 Almond milk
- ☐ 2 tbsp Coconut oil (melted, cooled)
- ☐ 1 tbsp Apple pie spice
- ☐ 1 tsp Ground Ceylon cinnamon
- ☐ 1/2 tsp Salt

FRUIT
- ☐ 2 Apples (peeled, grated)

OTHER
- ☐ 5 tbsp Filtered water

INSTRUCTIONS

- Combine the flaxseed meal and water, in a small dish. Leave the mixture alone for 10 to 15 minutes so that it can thicken.

- A baking sheet should be lined with parchment paper and the oven should be preheated to 350°F (175°C).
- Pour coconut oil over the nuts and coconut flakes in a single layer. Remove from the oven after 5-7 minutes and let cool.
- The oven's temperature should be raised to 375°F (190°C).
- To form a crumbly mixture, pulse nuts, and coconut in a food processor or powerful blender. Don't overprocess it or you'll end up with an oily combination.
- Combine the processed nuts, grated apples, almond milk, flaxseed mixture, extra coconut oil, spices, and salt in a large bowl. When the top starts to crisp and brown, transfer to a 9" x 9" (25 x 25 cm) baking dish and bake for 35 to 40 minutes.
- With warm coconut yogurt, serve.

Nutrition SERVING SIZE: 1
CALORIES: 335 FAT: 29g CHOLESTEROL: 0mg CARBOHYDRATES: 19g FIBER: 6g SUGAR: 10g PROTEIN: 6g

Breakfast Blues Porridge

Prep time: 5 minutes Serving 2
Ingredients
- ☐ ½ cup (50g) porridge oats
- ☐ ⅚ cup (200ml) milk
- ☐ ½ tsp vanilla extract
- ☐ 2 tbsp Greek yogurt

- ☐ ⅛ cup (25g) chia seeds
- ☐ ¾ cup (150g) blueberries
- ☐ ⅓ cup (25g) flaked almonds

Instructions

- Greek yogurt, chia seeds, milk, vanilla essence, and porridge oats are combined in a bowl and let to soak for a minute. Add some of the blueberries once the oats have softened.
- Add any leftover berries and almonds to the mixture before dividing it into two dishes.

Nutrition Per serve

Calories 347| Protein 15g| Carbs 42g| Fat 15g

Tomato and Watermelon Salad

Prep time + cook time: 5 minutes serving 2

Ingredients

- ☐ 1 tbsp olive oil
- ☐ 1 tbsp red wine vinegar
- ☐ ¼ tsp chili flakes

- ☐ 1 tbsp chopped mint
- ☐ ⅘ cup (120g) cherry tomatoes, chopped
- ☐ 1 ⅔ cups (250g) watermelon, cut into chunks
- ☐ ⅔ cup (100g) feta cheese, crumbled

Instructions

- To make the dressing, Season after combining the oil, vinegar, chili flakes, and mint.
- Place the watermelon and tomatoes in a bowl. Pour the dressing on top, stir in the feta, and then serve.

Nutrition Per serve
Calories 177| Protein 5g| Carbs 13g| Fat 13g

Smoothie with protein powder

Prep time 5 minutes cook time: 5 minutes serving 1
Ingredients

- ☐ 1 cup frozen berries
- ☐ 1 banana
- ☐ 1 cup unsweetened almond milk

☐ 1 scoop vanilla protein powder

Instructions
- To make everything smooth, combine all the ingredients in a blender

Nutrition Per serve
Calories 300| Protein 20g | Carbs 45g| Fat 5g| Fiber 5g

Greek yogurt with fruit and granola

Prep time + cook time: 5 minutes serving 21
Ingredients
☐ 1 cup plain Greek yogurt
☐ 1/2 cup berries
(such as blueberries, raspberries, or strawberries)
☐ 1/4 cup granola
(homemade or store-bought)

Instructions
- In a bowl, combine the Greek yogurt, berries, and granola.
- Serve immediately.

Nutrition Per serve
Calories 250| Protein 20g | Carbs 35g| Fat 10g| Fiber 5g

Whole-wheat toast with avocado

Prep time 5 minutes cook time: 5 minutes serving 1
Ingredients
- ☐ 1 slice of whole-wheat bread
- ☐ 1/2 avocado, mashed
- ☐ 1/4 teaspoon salt
- ☐ 1/8 teaspoon black pepper

Optional toppings: red pepper flakes, chives, or a egg

Instructions
- Toast the bread.
- Spread the mashed avocado on the toast.
- Sprinkle it with salt and pepper.
- Top with optional toppings

Nutrition Per serve
Calories 250| Protein 5g | Carbs 25g| Fat 15g| Fiber 5g

Hard-boiled eggs

Prep time 5 minutes cook time: 10 minutes serving 6
Ingredients
6 large eggs

Instructions:
- Boiling water in a large pot.
- Gently place the eggs into the boiling water using a slotted spoon.
- Cook the eggs for 6 to 8 minutes, or until they are done to your preference.
- To halt the cooking procedure, place the eggs right away in a dish of icy water.
- Serve the eggs after peeling them.

Nutrition Per serve
Calories 78| Protein 6g | Carbs 0g| Fat 5g| Fiber 0g

Yogurt parfait

Prep time 10 minutes cook time: 0 minutes serving 1
Ingredients
- ☐ 1/2 cup plain Greek yogurt
- ☐ 1/4 cup granola (choose a low-sugar option)
- ☐ 1/4 cup mixed berries
  (such as strawberries, blueberries, or raspberries)
- ☐ 1 tablespoon chopped nuts
  (such as almonds or walnuts)
- ☐ 1 teaspoon honey (optional, for added sweetness)

Instructions:
- In a serving glass or bowl, start by layering half of the Greek yogurt at the bottom.
- Add half of the granola on top of the yogurt layer.
- Layer half of the mixed berries on top of the granola.
- Repeat the layers with the remaining Greek yogurt, granola, and mixed berries.
- Sprinkle the chopped nuts over the final layer of berries.
- Drizzle honey on top, if desired, for added sweetness.
- Serve immediately and enjoy!

Nutrition Per Serve:
Calories: 250 Protein: 18g Fat: 9g Carbohydrates: 26g Fiber: 4g

Overnight oats

Servings: 1 Prep Time: 5 minutes Cook Time: 0 minutes Chill Time: 4-6 hours or overnight

Ingredients

- ☐ 1/2 cup rolled oats
- ☐ 1/2 cup unsweetened almond milk
  (or any other plant-based milk)
- ☐ 1/4 cup plain Greek yogurt
  (optional for added creaminess and protein)
- ☐ 1 tablespoon chia seeds
- ☐ 1/2 teaspoon vanilla extract
- ☐ 1/2 cup mixed berries
  (such as blueberries, strawberries, or raspberries)
- ☐ 1 tablespoon chopped nuts
  (such as almonds or walnuts)
- ☐ 1 teaspoon honey or maple syrup
  (optional, for added sweetness)

Instructions

- In a mason jar or container with a tight-fitting lid, combine the rolled oats, almond milk, Greek yogurt (if using), chia seeds, and vanilla

extract. Stir everything together carefully to make sure it's completely combined.
- On top of the oat mixture, sprinkle the mixed berries.
- Close the container tightly and refrigerate for at least 4-6 hours or overnight to allow the oats to soften and absorb the liquid.
- Before serving, give the oats a good stir. If the consistency is too thick, you may thin it down by adding a little bit of almond milk.
- Top with chopped nuts for added crunch and drizzle with honey or maple syrup if you prefer a sweeter taste.
- Enjoy!

Nutrition Per serve
Calories: 300/Protein: 14g/Fat: 10g/Carbohydrates: 40g/Fiber: 8g

Egg muffins

Servings: 4 Prep Time: 10 minutes Cook Time: 20 minutes
Ingredients
- ☐ 6 large eggs
- ☐ 1/2 cup diced vegetables
  (such as Bell peppers, spinach, onions, or mushrooms)

- ☐ 1/4 cup shredded cheese (such as cheddar or feta)
- ☐ Salt and pepper to taste
- ☐ Olive oil or cooking spray

Instructions:

- Preheat your oven to 350°F (175°C) and lightly grease a muffin tin with cooking spray or olive oil.
- Add salt and pepper to the beaten eggs before beating them in a small bowl.
- Add the diced vegetables and shredded cheese to the bowl, and mix everything together.
- Fill each cup in the muffin tray equally with the egg mixture, approximately 3/4 full.
- Bake in the preheated oven for approximately 18-20 minutes or until the egg muffins are set and slightly golden on top.
- Remove them from the oven and let them cool for a few minutes before removing them from the muffin tin.
- Serve the egg muffins warm or refrigerate them for later use. For up to four days, they may be kept in the refrigerator in an airtight container.
- Enjoy!

Nutrition (per serving):

Calories: 140 Protein: 11g Fat: 9g Carbohydrates: 2g Fiber: 2g

Breakfast burrito

Servings: 2 Prep Time: 10 minutes Cook Time:10minutes
Ingredients:
- ☐ 4 small whole wheat tortillas
- ☐ 4 large eggs
- ☐ 1/2 cup diced vegetable
  (such as bell peppers, onions, and spinach)
- ☐ 1/4 cup shredded cheese
  (such as cheddar or Monterey Jack)
- ☐ Salt and pepper to taste
- ☐ Cooking spray or olive oil for cooking

Instructions
- In the small skillet, crack the egg and season it with salt and pepper.
- Cooking spray or olive oil should be sparingly applied to a non-stick pan before heating it up over medium heat.
- Add the diced vegetables to the skillet and sauté until they are tender, about 3-4 minutes.
- Pour the beaten eggs into the opposite half of the pan while pushing the vegetables to one side.
- Scramble the eggs until cooked through, mixing them with the sautéed vegetables.

- Warm the tortillas in a separate pan or in the microwave for a few seconds until they are pliable.
- Divide the scrambled eggs and vegetable mixture evenly among the tortillas.
- Sprinkle shredded cheese over the eggs.
- Roll up each tortilla tightly, folding in the sides as you go.
- Optional: You can heat the assembled burritos in a pan for a few minutes to melt the cheese and make them warm and crispy.
- Serve the breakfast burritos warm and enjoy!

Nutrition (per serving):
Calories: 350| Protein: 20g|Fat: 15g|Carbohydrates: 30g|Fiber: 5g

Breakfast Sandwich

Servings: 1 Prep Time: 5 minutes Cook Time: 10 minutes
Ingredients:
- ☐ 1 whole wheat English muffin
- ☐ 1 large egg
- ☐ 1 slice of turkey bacon or turkey sausage patty
- ☐ 1 slice of tomato
- ☐ 1 slice of avocado

- ☐ Handful of spinach leaves
- ☐ Salt and pepper to taste
- ☐ Cooking spray or olive oil for cooking

Instructions:

- Preheat a non-stick skillet over medium heat and lightly coat it with cooking spray or olive oil.
- Cook the turkey bacon or turkey sausage patty according to the package instructions.
- In the same skillet, crack the egg and season it with salt and pepper.
- Cook the egg to your desired doneness, either scrambled or as a sunny-side-up or over-easy egg.
- While the egg is cooking, toast the whole wheat English muffin.
- Once toasted, spread the avocado on one-half of the English muffin.
- Layer the cooked egg, turkey bacon or sausage patty, tomato slice, and spinach leaves on the other half of the English muffin.
- Bring both halves together to form a delicious breakfast sandwich.
- Optionally, you can warm the assembled sandwich in the skillet for a few seconds to melt the cheese and make it warm and crispy.
- Serve the breakfast sandwich immediately and enjoy!

Nutrition Per Serve:
Calories: 300|Protein: 18g|Fat: 14g|Carbohydrates: 27g|Fiber: 6g

Lunch

Salad With Grilled Chicken or Fish

Servings: 1 Prep Time: 10 minutes Cook Time: 15 minutes

Ingredients:
- ☐ 1 small chicken breast or fish fillet (such as salmon or tilapia)
- ☐ Salt and pepper to taste
- ☐ 2 cups mixed salad greens (such as spinach, lettuce, or arugula)
- ☐ 1/2 cup cherry tomatoes, halved
- ☐ 1/4 cup sliced cucumber
- ☐ 1/4 cup sliced bell peppers
- ☐ 1/4 cup sliced red onions
- ☐ 1 tablespoon chopped fresh herbs (such as basil, cilantro, or parsley)
- ☐ 1 tablespoon extra-virgin olive oil
- ☐ 1 tablespoon balsamic vinegar or lemon juice

Optional toppings: sliced avocado,
roasted nuts or seeds,
crumbled feta cheese

Instructions
- Over medium heat, preheat a grill or grill pan.
- Salt and pepper the chicken breast or fish fillet on both sides.
- Grill the fish fillet or chicken breast for 6 to 8 minutes on each side, or until thoroughly cooked and beautifully charred. The thickness of the protein will influence how long it takes to cook.
- The chicken breast or fish fillet should be taken from the grill and given some time to rest before being cut into strips or cubes.
- Salad greens, cherry tomatoes, cucumber, bell peppers, red onions, and fresh herbs should all be combined in a big dish.
- Extra virgin olive oil, balsamic vinegar, and lemon juice should be drizzled over the salad. Toss the ingredients well to coat them completely.
- Place the salad in a serving dish or platter.
- Add the grilled chicken or fish to the salad as a garnish.
- You may also choose to add extras like sliced avocado, roasted nuts or seeds, or crumbled feta cheese.
- Enjoy the salad right away after serving it.

Nutrition Per Serve
Calories: 350 Protein: 25g Fat: 15-20g Carbohydrates: 20g Fiber: 7g

Soup

Servings: 4 Prep Time: 10 minutes Cook Time: 30 minutes

Ingredients:
- 1 tablespoon olive oil
- 1 onion, chopped
- 2 cloves garlic, minced
- 2 carrots, diced
- 2 celery stalks, diced
- 1 zucchini, diced
- 1 cup chopped seasonal vegetables
(such as broccoli, cauliflower, or bell peppers)
- 4 cups vegetable broth
- 1 cup cooked beans
(such as chickpeas or black beans)
- 1 cup canned diced tomatoes
- 1 teaspoon dried herbs
(such as thyme, oregano, or basil)
- Salt and pepper to taste
- **Optional toppings:** chopped fresh herbs ,
a squeeze of lemon juice,
or a drizzle of olive oil

Instructions:

1. In a big saucepan set over medium heat, warm the olive oil. When aromatic and transparent, add the minced garlic and diced onion.
2. Include the pot with the chopped carrots, celery, zucchini, and seasonal veggies. For a few minutes, stir and heat until slightly softened.
3. Add the broth made from vegetables, and then bring the mixture to a boil. Once the veggies are cooked, turn the heat down to low, cover the pot, and let it simmer for approximately 20 minutes.
4. Include canned chopped tomatoes and cooked beans in the saucepan. Add salt, pepper, and dry herbs as seasonings. Stir well, then simmer for a further ten minutes.
5. Turn off the heat and let the soup to gradually cool. If you want the soup to have a thicker consistency, purée a part of it using an immersion blender or a conventional blender.
6. Pour the soup into bowls and top with any toppings you choose, such as freshly chopped herbs, a squeeze of lemon juice, or a drizzle of olive oil.
7. Serve the soup hot and take a sip.

Nutrition Information (approximate values per serving):
- Calories: 150-200 Protein: 7g Fat: 6g Carbohydrates: 30g Fiber: 8g

Carrot, Orange and Avocado Salad

Prep time + cook time: 5 minutes serves 2
Ingredients

- ☐ 1 orange, plus zest and juice of 1
- ☐ 2 carrots, halved lengthways and sliced with a peeler
- ☐ 35g / 1 ½ cups rocket / arugula
- ☐ 1 avocado, stoned, peeled and sliced
- ☐ 1 tbsp olive oil

Instructions

- Sliced orange segments are added to a dish of avocado, carrots, rocket, and arugula. Orange juice, zest, and oil are combined in a bowl. Season the salad as you toss it.

Nutrition
Calories 177 Protein 5g Carbs 13g Fat 13g

Panzanella Salad

Prep time + cook time: 10 minutes serves 2
Ingredients

- ☐ 2 cups (300g) cherry tomatoes, chopped
- ☐ 1 garlic clove, crushed
- ☐ 1 tbsp capers, drained and rinsed
- ☐ 1 avocado, stoned, peeled and chopped
- ☐ 1 small red onion, very thinly sliced
- ☐ 2 slices of brown bread
- ☐ 2 tbsp olive oil
- ☐ 1 tbsp red wine vinegar
- ☐ small handful basil leaves

Instructions

- The tomatoes should be cut up and placed in a basin. Garlic, capers, avocado, and onion are added after a thorough seasoning. Mix well, then pause for ten minutes.
- In the meanwhile, rip the bread into pieces and put them in a basin. Pour half of the vinegar and half of the olive oil on top. Sprinkle tomatoes and basil leaves on top when you're ready to serve, then add the last of the oil and vinegar. Before serving, stir.

Nutrition per serve

Calories 452 Protein 6g Carbs 37g Fat 25g

Sandwich on whole-wheat bread with lean protein and vegetables

Servings: 1 Prep Time: 10 minutes Cook Time: 0 minutes
Ingredients:
- ☐ 2 slices of whole-wheat bread
- ☐ 3-4 ounces of lean protein
  (such as turkey breast, chicken breast, or tofu)
- ☐ 1/4 avocado, sliced
- ☐ 1/4 cup sliced cucumber
- ☐ 1/4 cup sliced bell peppers
- ☐ 1/4 cup baby spinach or lettuce leaves
- ☐ Mustard or low-fat mayonnaise (optional)
- ☐ Salt and pepper to taste

Instruction
- The two pieces of whole-wheat bread should be spread out on a spotless surface.
- If desired, spread low-fat mayonnaise or mustard on one or both pieces of bread.
- On one piece of bread, layer the lean protein (turkey breast, chicken breast, or tofu).

- Sliced avocado, cucumber, bell peppers, and spinach or lettuce leaves may be added as garnishes
- Add salt and pepper to the meal as desired
- To make a sandwich, put the second piece of bread on top.
- If preferred, cut the sandwich in half or quarters.
- You may either serve it now or save it for later.

Nutrition Per Serve
Calories: 350 g Protein: 30g Fat: 15g Carbohydrates: 35g Fiber: 8g

Tuna salad sandwich

Servings: 1 Prep Time: 10 minutes Cook Time: 0 minutes
Ingredients:
- ☐ 1 can of tuna in water (5 ounces)
- ☐ 2 tablespoons of low-fat Greek yogurt
- ☐ 1 tablespoon of light mayonnaise
- ☐ 1 tablespoon of lemon juice
- ☐ 1/4 cup of diced celery
- ☐ 1/4 cup of diced red onion
- ☐ 1/4 cup of diced pickles (optional)
- ☐ Salt and pepper to taste
- ☐ 2 slices of whole-wheat bread

- ☐ Lettuce leaves
- ☐ sliced tomatoes

Instructions

- Tuna in a can should be drained of water and placed in a mixing dish.
- Celery, red onion, pickles (if used), light mayonnaise, lemon juice, and low-fat Greek yogurt should all be added to the dish.
- All the components should be well mixed.
- Add salt and pepper to the meal as desired
- If preferred, toast the two pieces of whole wheat bread.
- One piece of bread should be properly spread with the tuna salad mixture.
- Slices of tomato and lettuce should be added on top.
- To make a sandwich, put the second piece of bread on top.
- If preferred, cut the sandwich in half or quarters.
- You may either serve it now or save it for later.

Nutrition Per Serve

Calories: 350 Protein: 30g Fat: 8g Carbohydrates: 30g Fiber: 6g

Chicken Salad Sandwich

Servings: 1 Prep Time: 15 minutes Cook Time: 15 minutes
Ingredients:

- ☐ 4 ounces of cooked chicken breast diced
- ☐ 2 tablespoons of low-fat Greek yogurt
- ☐ 1 tablespoon of light mayonnaise
- ☐ 1 teaspoon of Dijon mustard
- ☐ 1/4 cup of diced celery
- ☐ 1/4 cup of diced red onion
- ☐ 1/4 cup of diced apple (optional)
- ☐ Salt and pepper to taste
- ☐ 2 slices of whole-wheat bread
- ☐ Lettuce leaves
- ☐ sliced tomatoes for garnish

Instructions:
- Cook the chicken breast completely by grilling, roasting, or boiling it. After allowing it to cool, chop or dice it.
- Chicken that has been shredded or diced, low-fat Greek yogurt, light mayonnaise, Dijon mustard, celery, red onion, and chopped apple (if used) should all be combined in a mixing dish.
- All the components should be well mixed.
- Add salt and pepper to the meal as desired
- If preferred, toast the two pieces of whole wheat bread.
- One piece of bread should be properly spread with the chicken salad mixture.
- Slices of tomato and lettuce should be added on top.
- To make a sandwich, put the second piece of bread on top.
- If preferred, cut the sandwich in half or quarters.
- You may either serve it now or save it for later.

Nutrition per serves
Calories: 400 Protein: 30g Fat: 8g Carbohydrates: 35g Fiber: 6g

Quinoa bowl with black beans, corn, and salsa

Servings: 2 Prep Time: 10 minutes Cook Time: 20 minutes

Ingredients:
- ☐ 1 cup of cooked quinoa
- ☐ 1 can (15 ounces) of black beans,
- ☐ rinsed and drained
- ☐ 1 cup of corn kernels (fresh or frozen)
- ☐ 1/2 cup of salsa
  (choose a low-sodium option)
- ☐ 1/4 cup of chopped fresh cilantro
- ☐ Juice of 1 lime
- ☐ Salt and pepper to taste

Optional toppings: avocado slices,
diced tomatoes,
sliced green onions

Instructions
- Quinoa should be prepared per the directions on the box, then put aside.
- A little amount of olive oil should be heated over medium heat in a big skillet.

- The corn kernels should be slightly browned and soft after 3–4 minutes of cooking in the pan. Get rid of the heat.
- Combine the cooked quinoa, black beans, corn, salsa, cilantro, lime juice, salt, and pepper in a mixing bowl. Blend well.
- If necessary, taste and adjust the seasoning.
- Divide the quinoa mixture into two dishes for serving.
- Add extra toppings to each bowl, such as chopped tomatoes, avocado slices, and green onion slices.
- Serve right away and delight.

Nutrition per serves
Calories: 400 Protein: 15g Fat: 3g Carbohydrates: 70g Fiber: 10g

Tofu stir-fry

Servings: 2 Prep Time: 15 minutes Cook Time: 15minutes
Ingredients
- ☐ 8 ounces of firm tofu,
- ☐ drained and cubed
- ☐ 2 tablespoons of low-sodium soy sauce
- ☐ 1 tablespoon of sesame oil
- ☐ 1 tablespoon of cornstarch
- ☐ 1 tablespoon of olive oil

- ☐ 1 garlic clove, minced
- ☐ 1 small onion, sliced
- ☐ 1 bell pepper, sliced
- ☐ 1 cup of broccoli florets
- ☐ 1 cup of sliced mushrooms
- ☐ 1 cup of snap peas
- ☐ Salt and pepper to taste

Optional toppings: sesame seeds, chopped green onions

Instructions:

- Cornstarch, soy sauce, and sesame oil should all be combined in a dish. Toss the tofu cubes in the mixture carefully to coat. 10 minutes should be set up for marinating.
- In a large skillet or wok set over medium-high heat, warm the olive oil.
- Sliced onion and minced garlic are added to the pan and cooked for two to three minutes, or until aromatic and just starting to soften.
- When the tofu is brown and crispy on the exterior, add the marinated tofu and simmer for 5–6 minutes, turning once or twice.
- To the pan, add the bell pepper, broccoli florets, thinly sliced mushrooms, and snap peas. Stir-fry the veggies for a further 4-5 minutes, or until they are crisp-tender.
- Add salt and pepper to the meal as desired
- If preferred, sprinkle with chopped green onions and sesame seeds after removing from the heat.
- Serve the tofu stir-fry hot over quinoa or steamed rice.

Nutrition per serves

Calories: 390 Protein: 15g Fat: 12g Carbohydrates: 20g Fiber: 5g

Veggie wrap

Servings: 2 Prep Time: 15 minutes Cook Time: 0 minutes

Ingredients

- ☐ 2 large whole-wheat tortilla wraps
- ☐ 1/2 cup hummus
- ☐ 1 cup mixed salad greens
- ☐ 1/2 cup sliced cucumber
- ☐ 1/2 cup sliced bell peppers
- ☐ 1/2 cup shredded carrots
- ☐ 1/4 cup sliced red onion
- ☐ 1/4 cup sliced avocado
- ☐ Salt and pepper to taste

Instructions:

- On a spotless surface, spread the tortilla wrappers out.
- Each wrap should be liberally spread with hummus.
- The two wraps should be filled with equal amounts of mixed salad greens, cucumber slices, bell pepper slices, shredded carrots, red onion, and avocado slices.
- To taste, season with salt and pepper.

- To make a wrap that is secure, fold the edges of the wraps in before securely rolling them up from one end.
- If needed, cut the wraps in half diagonally to make handling simpler.
- To pack the vegetable wraps for meals on the go, wrap them in foil or parchment paper before serving.

Nutrition per serves
Calories: 300 Protein: 8g Fat: 10g Carbohydrates: 35g Fiber: 8g

Salad with chickpeas

Servings: 2 Prep Time: 15 minutes Cook Time: 0minutes
Ingredients
- ☐ 4 cups mixed salad greens
- ☐ 1 cup cooked chickpeas (canned or homemade)
- ☐ 1/2 cup cherry tomatoes, halved
- ☐ 1/2 cup cucumber, diced
- ☐ 1/4 cup red onion, thinly sliced
- ☐ 1/4 cup Kalamata olives,
- ☐ pitted and halved
- ☐ 2 tablespoons chopped fresh parsley
- ☐ 2 tablespoons extra-virgin olive oil
- ☐ 1 tablespoon lemon juice
- ☐ 1/2 teaspoon dried oregano
- ☐ Salt and pepper to taste

Instructions:
- Salad greens, cooked chickpeas, cherry tomatoes, cucumber, red onion, Kalamata olives, and chopped parsley should all be combined in a big salad dish.
- Mix the olive oil, lemon juice, dried oregano, salt, and pepper to prepare the dressing in a small basin.
- The salad should be well-dressed once the dressing has been drizzled over it.
- If necessary, taste and make seasoning adjustments.
- On two plates or bowls, divide the salad.
- Enjoy serving right away.

Nutrition per serves
Calories: 350 Protein: 10g Fat: 14g Carbohydrates: 35g Fiber: 10g

Swiss Chard Quiche

Servings: 6 Prep Time: 25minutes CookTime: 25 minutes
Ingredients
PROTEIN
- ☐ 12 oz Bacon
   (or pork belly, diced)
- ☐ 10 Eggs

PANTRY

- ☐ 2 tbsp Olive oil
- ☐ 1/3 cup Canned coconut milk
- ☐ 3/4 tsp Salt
- ☐ 1/4 tsp Black pepper

VEGETABLE
- ☐ 3 cup Swiss chard (stems removed, roughly chopped)
- ☐ 1 Zucchini (diced)
- ☐ 1 Onion (diced)

INSTRUCTIONS
- Grease a 10" (25 cm) pie dish with olive oil and preheat your oven to 350°F (180°C).
- The bacon and onions should be fried for 7 to 10 minutes in a little amount of olive oil in a large pan over medium heat before being transferred to the pie plate. As much fat as you can keep in the pan will help the veggies cook.
- While the skillet is still hot, add the zucchini and Swiss chard, and sauté until tender. Transferring with caution, be sure to keep any extra water in the skillet.
- Mix the eggs, coconut milk, salt, and pepper in a large bowl. Pour over the bacon and vegetables into the dish.
- The egg needs 30 minutes in the oven to completely set.
- Before serving with hollandaise sauce, nutritional yeast, spicy sauce, or sugar-free ketchup, let it cool for 15 minutes.
- Any leftovers should be kept in the refrigerator for up to four days in a tightly sealed container.

NUTRITION SERVING SIZE: 1
CALORIES:478 FAT: 35g CHOLESTEROL: 366mg CARBOHYDRATES: 8g FIBER: 2g SUGAR: 3g PROTEIN: 32g

Asian Chicken Slaw

Servings: 6 Prep Time: 1 hour Cook Time: 1 hour
Ingredients

PROTEIN
- ☐ 2 lb Chicken thighs (boneless)

PANTRY
- ☐ 1 tsp Garlic powder
- ☐ 1 tsp Onion powder
- ☐ 2 tsp Paprika
- ☐ 1 tsp Salt
- ☐ 3 tbsp Coconut oil
- ☐ 1 Whole star anise
- ☐ 1/2 cup Apple cider vinegar
- ☐ 3/4 cup Olive oil
- ☐ 1 tbsp Sesame oil
- ☐ 2 tbsp Coconut aminos
- ☐ 1/2 cup Almonds (chopped)
- ☐ 1.5 cup Cooked quinoa

VEGETABLES
- ☐ 1 Chinese cabbage (cored, thinly sliced)
- ☐ 2 Carrots (julienned)
- ☐ 1/8 Red cabbage (cored, thinly sliced)
- ☐ 2 cup Sugar snap peas

(roughly chopped)
- ☐ 1 tsp Ginger
(finely chopped - for the vegetables)
- ☐ 1 tsp Ginger
(grated - for the dressing)
- ☐ 1 tsp Garlic (minced)
- ☐ 2 Scallions
(chopped, greens and whites separated

INSTRUCTIONS

- Chicken preparation: Salt, paprika, garlic powder, onion powder, and other seasonings should be added to the chicken before baking, grilling, or frying it. After allowing it cool, chop or shred it into bite-sized pieces.
- The star anise, minced garlic, white part of the scallions, finely sliced ginger, and lots of coconut oil should be sautéed in the pan with the veggies. They may emit their scent in around 30 seconds. Once you've finished, discard the star anise.
- Add the carrots and Chinese cabbage, both of which have been thinly sliced, and gently mix the veggies until they start to soften. It is recommended to sauté the veggies for no more than a few minutes since the shorter the cooking time, the crispier they will be. Add to a large mixing bowl when finished.
- Get the dressing ready: In a small bowl, mix the grated ginger, coconut aminos, olive oil, sesame oil, and apple cider vinegar.
- Put everything together: Add the thinly sliced purple cabbage, sugar snap peas, slivered almonds, cooked quinoa, and chicken to the large dish holding the sautéed veggies. Add the dressing on top, then quickly toss.
- Keep the dressing separate if you want to serve this meal over many days and use it shortly before serving. This will prevent the slaw from becoming mushy.

NUTRITION SERVING SIZE: 1

CALORIES:814 FAT:64g CHOLESTEROL:194g CARBOHYDRATES: 21g
FIBER: 5g SUGAR: 5g PROTEIN: 42g

Sweet Potato Noodle Salad

Servings: 4 PrepTime: 15 minutes CookTime: 20 minutes
Ingredients

PANTRY
- ☐ 1/2 cup Olive oil
- ☐ 1/2 cup Pepitas
- ☐ 1/2 tsp Chili powder
- ☐ 1/2 tsp Salt

VEGETABLES
- ☐ 16 oz Sweet potato/yam
- ☐ 2 Corn on the cob (cut kernels off cob)
- ☐ 1 cup Fresh cilantro/coriander (chopped)
- ☐ 4 cup Baby spinach
- ☐ 1 tsp Garlic (minced)

FRUIT
- ☐ 1 Orange (juiced)
- ☐ 2 tbsp Lemon juice

INSTRUCTIONS

- A skillet should be heated to medium. The sweet potato noodles should be fried in copious amounts of olive oil, flipping after a few minutes, until they are no longer stiff. You don't want them to get mushy, so be cautious not to overcook them either. You should be good to go in around 5 minutes. Take out the noodles and place them in a big bowl.
- Spin the tiny spinach leaves in the pan briskly to wilt them. You just need to slightly lower the amount of cooking since less is better. In the dish with the noodles, put the spinach.
- Return the skillet to the fire after cleaning and drying it. Sweet corn may be roasted by letting it brown on a hot pan without disturbing it. Only throw them one every few minutes till you're done.
- Corn, cilantro, and pepitas should all be added to the dish of noodles.
- Combine olive oil, chili powder, garlic, orange juice, lemon juice, and salt to make the dressing. Completely combine.
- Top the salad with the dressing and toss it around to evenly coat it.
- It's preferable to keep the dressing separate until you're ready to eat if you want to consume this salad across multiple meals.

NUTRITION: SERVING SIZE: 1
CALORIES: 543 FAT: 35g CARBOHYDRATES: 52g FIBER: 9g

Dinner

Pulled Pork

Servings: 8 Prep Time: 10 minutes Cook Time: 20 minutes

Ingredients

PANTRY
- ☐ 3 lb Pork butt
- ☐ 14 oz Canned diced tomatoes
- ☐ 1/2 cup Tomato paste
- ☐ 3 tbsp Apple cider vinegar
- ☐ 1 tbsp Ground cumin
- ☐ 2 tsp Ground Ceylon cinnamon
- ☐ 1 tbsp Paprika
- ☐ 1 tsp Fennel seeds
- ☐ 1 tsp Salt
- ☐ 1 tsp Black pepper

VEGETABLES
- ☐ 8 oz Potatoes (cut into 1/2" pieces)
- ☐ 2 Onions (diced)
- ☐ 2 tbsp Garlic (minced)

INSTRUCTIONS

- To the Crockpot, add the potatoes, onions, and pork butt.
- Pour the other ingredients, which have been combined in a jug or basin, over and around the pig butt.
- Cook the beef on low for 8 to 10 hours, or until it is tender and soft to shred with a fork. The cook time should be extended by a few hours when cooking from frozen.
- Once finished, shred the pulled pork and combine it with the sauce and seasonings.

NUTRITION SERVING SIZE: 1
CALORIES:529 FAT:33g CARBOHYDRATES:16g FIBER:4g SUGAR: 5g
PROTEIN: 42g

Creamy Tomato Baked Fish

Servings:4 Prep Time: 25mins Cook Time: 20 mins

INGREDIENTS
PROTEIN
- ☐ 28 oz Fish fillet

PANTRY
- ☐ 28 oz Canned crushed tomatoes
- ☐ 3/4 cup Canned coconut milk

- ☐ 1 tsp Dried oregano
- ☐ 1 tsp Dried basil
- ☐ 1/2 tsp Red pepper flakes
- ☐ 1 tsp Salt
- ☐ 1/2 tsp Black pepper

VEGETABLE
- ☐ 1 tsp Garlic (minced)
- ☐ 5 cup Cauliflower (riced)
- ☐ 2 Tomatoes (sliced 1/4" thick)
- ☐ 2 cup Butternut squash (diced into 1/2" cubes)
- ☐ 1/2 cup Fresh basil

INSTRUCTIONS

- Set the oven's temperature to 425°F (220°C).
- Crushed tomatoes, coconut milk, dried basil, oregano, red pepper flakes, salt, and pepper should all be combined in a big bowl. Mix thoroughly.
- Pre-cook the riced cauliflower for 5 minutes in the microwave or on the stove.
- Riced cauliflower that has been cooked; add to cheesecloth or nut milk bag; squeeze out as much moisture as you can.
- In a large baking dish, add the cauliflower rice and then arrange the fresh tomatoes on top of it. Layer the squash on top of the sauce after adding half of the tomato cream sauce. Add the fish fillets and then top with the remaining sauce.
- Bake the fish and squash for 20 minutes, or until they are both cooked through.
- Serve with fresh basil as a garnish.

NUTRITION: YIELD: 4 SERVING SIZE: 1
CALORIES:456 FAT:12g CHOLESTEROL:186mg CARBOHYDRATES: 36g FIBER: 12g SUGAR: 16g PROTEIN: 56g

Zambreros Burrito Bowl

PREP TIME: 45 MINS. Serves 4
INGREDIENTS
PROTEIN
- ☐ 22 oz Chicken thighs

PANTRY
- ☐ 2 tbsp Olive oil (for chicken)
- ☐ 2 tbsp Olive oil (for black beans)
- ☐ 15 oz Canned black beans (drained and rinsed)
- ☐ 1/8 tsp Chili powder
- ☐ 1/2 tsp Ground cumin
- ☐ 1/2 tsp Paprika
- ☐ 1/4 tsp Garlic powder
- ☐ 1/2 tsp Dried onion
- ☐ 1/4 tsp Dried oregano
- ☐ 1 tsp Salt
- ☐ 1/8 tsp Pepper
- ☐ 2 tbsp Salsa

VEGETABLE
- ☐ 2 cup Romaine (Cos) lettuce (sliced finely)

- ☐ 4 Corn on the cob
- ☐ 4 Tomatoes (diced)
- ☐ 1/2 cup Fresh cilantro/coriander

FRUIT
- ☐ 2 Avocados (diced)
- ☐ 1 Lime (juiced)

INSTRUCTIONS

- To fully cook the chicken, bake, grill, or fry it.
- Make the seasoning while the chicken is roasting. Combine chili powder, cumin, paprika, garlic powder, onion powder, oregano, salt, and pepper in a small basin or bottle.
- When the chicken is finished cooking, place it on a platter and shred it with a fork.
- Re-add the chicken to the pan along with the spice mix, oil, and olives. Completely combine them before putting them away.
- In a small saucepan, cook the black beans for two to three minutes before seasoning with salt and olive oil.
- Diced avocados, salsa, lime juice, and a pinch of salt to taste are combined in a small dish to make guacamole. To get the desired texture, mash.
- On high, microwave the corn (husks included). Per corn, allow 4 minutes. Once finished, take off the husk. Cut the kernels off the cob while holding it vertically over a plate or a clean cutting board.
- Put together a vibrant platter with black beans, sweet corn, guacamole, fresh lettuce, and tomatoes along with seasoned chicken. Use cilantro as a garnish.

NUTRITION INFORMATION: YIELD: 4 SERVING SIZE: 1
CALORIES:844 FAT:52g CHOLESTEROL:200mg CARBOHYDRATES: 56g FIBER: 19g. SUGAR: 10g PROTEIN: 50g

Harvest Chicken Chili

PREP TIME: 15 MINS. COOK TIME: 6 HOURS
TOTAL TIME: 6 HOURS 15 MINS
INGREDIENTS
PROTEIN
- ☐ 22 oz Chicken breast

PANTRY
- ☐ 4 tbsp Olive oil
- ☐ 1 tsp Chili powder
- ☐ 2 tsp Paprika
- ☐ 1 tsp Ground cumin
- ☐ 1 tsp Garlic powder
- ☐ 1/8 tsp Cayenne pepper
- ☐ 1 tsp Salt
- ☐ 1 tsp Black pepper
- ☐ 1 cup Chicken stock
- ☐ 1 cup Pumpkin puree
- ☐ 15 oz Canned corn (drained)
- ☐ 15 oz Canned black beans (drained)

VEGETABLE
- ☐ 1 Onion (finely chopped)
- ☐ 2 Red bell peppers

(chopped into small pieces)

INSTRUCTIONS
- In a crockpot, combine all the ingredients except the canned corn and black beans. Cook for five hours on low.
- Cook for another hour or so after adding the tinned corn and black beans.
- After it is finished, shred the chicken and simmer it for a further 10 minutes to let it absorb some of the liquid.
- Ideally served over cauliflower rice and topped with avocado, cilantro, and other favorite toppings.

NUTRITION : YIELD: 4 SERVING SIZE: 1
CALORIES:625 FAT:22g CHOLESTEROL:134mg CARBOHYDRATES: 48g
FIBER: 13g SUGAR: 12g PROTEIN: 61g

Shrimp Fried Rice

**PREP TIME: 10 MINS. COOK TIME: 10 MINS.
TOTAL TIME: 20 MINUTES. SERVINGS 4
INGREDIENTS**
PROTEIN
- ☐ 20 oz Fresh shrimp (peeled, de-veined)

PANTRY
- ☐ 2 tbsp Coconut oil
- ☐ 3 tbsp Coconut aminos
- ☐ 3 tbsp Gluten-free tamari sauce
- ☐ 1 tbsp Fish sauce
- ☐ 1/4 tsp Salt

VEGETABLE
- ☐ 2 tsp Garlic (minced)
- ☐ 1 Onion (finely diced)
- ☐ 1 Zucchini (finely diced)
- ☐ 2 cup Mushroom (finely diced)
- ☐ 2 Carrots (finely diced)
- ☐ 6 cup Cauliflower (riced)
- ☐ 4 Scallions (chopped)

INSTRUCTIONS

- Warm the coconut oil in a large pan over medium heat. After adding, simmer the shrimp for 5 minutes.
- After removing the shrimp, mix in the garlic, onion, zucchini, mushrooms, and carrots for 5 minutes.
- Add the riced cauliflower to the skillet and cook for 5 minutes after removing the veggies from the pan. If extra coconut oil is required, add it.
- Add the cooked veggies and shrimp back into the pan after the cauliflower has been riced.
- Stir regularly for 2 minutes, and add the fish sauce, tamari, and coconut aminos. Make sure the shrimp and veggies are well-covered.
- Add salt to taste, add scallions as a garnish, and then serve hot.
- Refrigerate leftovers for up to three days in an airtight container.

NUTRITION YIELD: 4 SERVING SIZE: 1
CALORIES:317 FAT:9g CHOLESTEROL:268mg CARBOHYDRATES: 22g FIBER: 8g SUGAR: 11g PROTEIN: 42g

Zuppa Toscana

PREP TIME: 30 MINS   COOK TIME: 5 HOURS 30 MINS
TOTAL TIME: 6 HOURS.   SERVINGS 4
INGREDIENTS

PROTEIN
- ☐ 6 oz Bacon
- ☐ (cut into ½" pieces)
- ☐ 16 oz Chicken sausage (sliced)

PANTRY
- ☐ 1 tbsp Ghee
- ☐ 4 cup Chicken stock
- ☐ 1/2 tsp Red pepper flakes
- ☐ 2 tsp Italian herbs
- ☐ 13.5 fl oz Canned coconut milk

VEGETABLE
- ☐ 1 Onion (diced)
- ☐ 2 tbsp Garlic (minced)
- ☐ 8 oz Sweet potato/yam (diced into bite-sized pieces)
- ☐ 4 cup Kale (stems removed, leaves chopped)

INSTRUCTIONS

- Crispy bacon is cooked in a big pan that has been heated with some ghee.
- Add the chicken sausage to the same skillet still containing the bacon fat, and cook until browned.
- When the onions are transparent, add the garlic and onions and simmer for an additional 4-5 minutes.
- Add the contents of the skillet to the sweet potatoes in the slow cooker. Stir in the chicken stock, red pepper, Italian herbs, and a generous amount of salt to taste.
- Cook for 5 to 6 hours on low, or 3 hours on high, with the lid on.
- Kale and coconut milk are added, and the dish is covered and cooked for a further 15 minutes on high.
- Add the bacon, then season to taste with salt and pepper.

NUTRITION: YIELD: 4 SERVING SIZE: 1
CALORIES:869 FAT:54g CHOLESTEROL: 162mg CARBOHYDRATES: 44g FIBER: 6g SUGAR: 10g PROTEIN: 54g

Slow Cooked Beef and Broccoli

PREP TIME: 15 MINS. COOK TIME: 6 HOURS.
TOTAL TIME: 6 HOURS 15 MINS
INGREDIENTS
PROTEIN
- ☐ 22 oz Beef flank steaks

(sliced into strips against the grain)
PANTRY
- ☐ 1 cup Beef Stock
- ☐ 2 tbsp Coconut aminos
- ☐ 1/2 cup Gluten-free tamari sauce
- ☐ 2 tsp Sesame oil
- ☐ 1 tbsp White wine vinegar
- ☐ 1/2 tsp Chinese 5 spice powder
- ☐ 3 tbsp Arrowroot flour

VEGETABLES
- ☐ 1 Onion (diced)
- ☐ 4 tsp Garlic (minced)
- ☐ 2 tsp Ginger (minced)
- ☐ 3 Broccoli (cut into florets)

OTHER
- ☐ 1 tbsp Filtered water

INSTRUCTIONS

- [Optional] For a few minutes, sear the steak in a hot pan with coconut oil. The meat will stick together better and the taste will be more intense as a result.
- In a Crockpot (slow cooker), combine the beef, beef stock, coconut aminos, tamari sauce, sesame oil, white wine vinegar, Chinese five spice powder, onions, garlic, and ginger. Cook on low for 6 hours or on high for 3 to 4 hours after stirring everything together.
- Add the arrowroot flour to the Crockpot after dissolving it in a little amount of cold water just before serving. Stir in the broccoli after adding it.
- To enable the sauce to thicken and the broccoli to soften, simmer covered on low for an additional 10 to 15 minutes.
- Serve with cauliflower rice or red, black, or wild rice.

NUTRITION YIELD: 4 SERVING SIZE: 1
CALORIES:391 FAT:15g CHOLESTEROL:123mg CARBOHYDRATES: 13g FIBER: 1g SUGAR: 3g PROTEIN: 49g

Dessert

Chocolate Mud Cake

PREP TIME: 20 MINUTES. COOK TIME: 40 MINUTES
TOTAL TIME: 1 HOUR. Serves 6
INGREDIENTS
PROTEIN
- ☐ 6 Eggs
  (yolks and whites separated)

PANTRY
- ☐ 7 oz Dark chocolate
  (85% cacao) (chopped)
- ☐ 2/3 cup Coconut oil (melted)

For The cake
- ☐ 1/4 cup Cacao powder
- ☐ 3 tsp Rice malt syrup
- ☐ 1 1/2 cup Almond meal

For The icing
- ☐ 2 tbsp Cacao powder
- ☐ 1 cup Coconut cream

☐ 1 tsp Rice malt syrup

INSTRUCTIONS
- Making the cake:
- The oven should be heated to 340°F/170°C.
- An 8"/20cm cake pan should be greased and lined with parchment paper.
- Put a heat-resistant bowl over a saucepan of simmering water on the stove.
- Combine the cacao powder, coconut oil, and dark chocolate in that basin. Stirring until melted, separating, and let to cool.
- The egg yolks and rice malt syrup should be combined and beaten until thick and creamy in a separate mixing dish.
- After cooling, gently pour the chocolate mixture into the egg mixture and beat to blend.
- Beat in the almond meal after adding it.
- In a separate dish, whip the egg whites until soft peaks form.
- With a large spoon, fold one-third of the egg whites into the chocolate mixture before adding the remaining whites.
- Pour the mixture into the pan and bake for approximately 40 minutes, or until the middle feels dry to the touch and slightly springs back
- Making chocolate frosting involves:
- Place a heatproof bowl over a saucepan of simmering water on the stove.
- Combine the cacao powder, coconut cream, and rice malt syrup in the basin. until melted, stir.
- Spread it on the cake's top while it is still warm.
- The icing will become firmer after it has cooled or if it is refrigerated.

NUTRITION: YIELD: 6 SERVING SIZE: 1
CALORIES:861 FAT:62g CHOLESTEROL:189mg CARBOHYDRATES: 25g FIBER: 7g SUGAR: 10g PROTEIN: 16g

Banana Bread

**PREP TIME: 10 MINS.   COOK TIME: 40 MINS.
 TOTAL TIME: 50 MINS**
SERVES 6
INGREDIENTS
PROTEIN
- ☐ 2 Eggs

PANTRY
- ☐ 1 cup Almond butter
- ☐ 1 cup Almond meal
- ☐ 1 tsp Baking soda
- ☐ 1 tsp Baking powder

FRUIT
- ☐ 3 Bananas (very ripe)

INSTRUCTIONS
- Grease a loaf pan and preheat the oven to 350°F/180°C.
- Bananas should be mashed in a bowl with a fork.
- Add the almond butter, almond meal, and eggs.
- Add the baking soda and powder after everything has been well blended. Together nicely.
- Place a loaf pan with the ingredients in it and bake for 35 to 40 minutes.
- Use a toothpick to test the banana bread's doneness; if the toothpick emerges clean, the bread is done.

NUTRITION: YIELD: 6 SERVING SIZE: 1
CALORIES: 441 FAT:34g CHOLESTEROL:62mg CARBOHYDRATES: 26g FIBER: 8g SUGAR: 10g PROTEIN: 15g

Berry Delight

PREP TIME: 15 MINUTES.   COOK TIME: 35 MINUTES
TOTAL TIME: 50 MINUTES. SERVES 16
INGREDIENTS
PROTEIN
- ☐ 2 Eggs (room temperature)

PANTRY
- ☐ 2 cup Almond flour
- ☐ 2/3 cup Tapioca flour
- ☐ 1/3 cup Coconut flour
- ☐ 1 tsp Baking soda
- ☐ 1/2 tsp Salt
- ☐ 1/4 cup Almond milk
- ☐ 1/2 cup Rice malt syrup
- ☐ (or light corn syrup)
- ☐ 1/4 cup Coconut oil

- ☐ 1/2 tbsp Apple cider vinegar
- ☐ 1 tsp Vanilla extract

FRUIT
- ☐ 2 cup Fresh berries

INSTRUCTIONS

- A sheet pan should be greased and the oven set to 350°F (175°C). For a quantity of 12 servings, a 9 x 13" sheet pan (or 35 x 25 cm baking tray) works well.
- Almond flour, tapioca flour, coconut flour, baking soda, and salt should all be combined in a big basin.
- The eggs, almond milk, rice malt syrup, coconut oil, apple cider vinegar, and vanilla extract should all be combined in a different bowl.
- Mix thoroughly after adding the wet components to the basin containing the dry ingredients.
- Using a spatula, spread the batter into the prepared sheet pan and level it out.
- After topping the mixture with the berries, bake the cake for 30-35 minutes, or until brown.
- Slice and eat with a little coconut yogurt or whipped coconut cream after letting it cool.

NUTRITION: YIELD: 12 SERVING SIZE: 1
CALORIES:228 FAT:15g CHOLESTEROL:31mg CARBOHYDRATES: 18g
FIBER: 4g SUGAR: 4g PROTEIN: 6g

Ginger Cookies

PREP TIME: 10 MINS COOK TIME: 15 MINS
ADDITIONAL TIME: 2 HOURS
INGREDIENTS
PROTEIN
- ☐ 1 Egg

PANTRY
- ☐ 2.5 cup Almond meal
- ☐ 1/4 cup Coconut flour
- ☐ 1/2 tsp Salt
- ☐ 1/2 cup Rice malt syrup
- ☐ 1 tsp Ground Ceylon cinnamon
- ☐ 1 tbsp Ginger powder
- ☐ 1 tsp Ground cloves
- ☐ 1 tsp Baking powder
- ☐ 1 tbsp Orange zest
- ☐ 1 tsp Vanilla extract
- ☐ 4 tbsp Ghee

INSTRUCTIONS
- Pulse the almond meal, coconut flour, salt, herbs, and baking powder in a food processor.
- When the dough begins to form a ball, add the additional ingredients and pulse.

- Refrigerate the dough for two hours after wrapping it in plastic wrap.
- When you are prepared to bake, preheat the oven to 180°C or 350°C and line a baking sheet with parchment paper.
- The dough should yield around 16 cookies when it is flattened and formed into little balls.
- 15 minutes or until the rims are golden brown should be spent baking.

NUTRITION YIELD: 16 SERVING SIZE: 1
CALORIES:156 FAT:13g CHOLESTEROL:20mg CARBOHYDRATES: 8g FIBER: 3g SUGAR: 2g PROTEIN: 5g

Chai Tea Frozen Yogurt

PREP TIME: 10 MINS   ADDITIONAL TIME: 3 HOURS
INGREDIENTS
- ☐ 13.5 oz Canned coconut milk
- ☐ 2 cup Coconut yogurt
- ☐ 1 cup Shredded coconut
- ☐ 4 Chai tea bags
- ☐ 1 tsp Ground Ceylon cinnamon

INSTRUCTIONS
- Pour just enough hot, boiling water over the chai tea bags in a coffee cup to cover them. For up to five minutes, steep.

- In a high-speed blender, combine the coconut milk, coconut yogurt, coconut shreds, and cinnamon. Blend on high until smooth. As necessary, scrape the blender's sides.
- Pour the chai tea into the blender after you squeeze and remove the tea bags. Use a spoon to mix by hand or blend on low.
- The mixture should be frozen for 3 to 4 hours before a quick low-speed mixing.
- Take a spoonful from each dish after dividing.

NUTRITION: YIELD: 6 SERVING SIZE: 1
CALORIES:266 FAT:18g CHOLESTEROL:2mg CARBOHYDRATES: 25g
FIBER: 2g SUGAR: 20g PROTEIN: 5g

Spiced Nut Muffins

PREP TIME: 35 MINS   COOK TIME: 25 MINS   Seves 12
INGREDIENTS
PROTEIN
- ☐ 2 Eggs

PANTRY
- ☐ 1 cup Gluten-free baking flour (all-purpose)
- ☐ 1/2 cup Buckwheat flour
- ☐ 1 1/2 tsp Baking powder
- ☐ 1 tsp Ground nutmeg

- ☐ 2 tsp Ground Ceylon cinnamon (for batter)
- ☐ 1/2 cup Pecans (roughly chopped - for batter)
- ☐ 1/2 cup Almond milk
- ☐ 1/2 cup Ghee
- ☐ 2 tsp Vanilla extract
- ☐ 1 cup Pumpkin puree
- ☐ 1/4 cup Pecans (roughly chopped - for topping)
- ☐ 2 tbsp Sunflower seeds
- ☐ 2 tbsp Pepitas
- ☐ 2 tbsp Shredded coconut
- ☐ 1 tsp Ground Ceylon cinnamon (for topping)

INSTRUCTIONS

- The oven should be heated to 350°F (180°C). A 12-cup muffin tray should be lightly greased or lined with baking paper.
- In a large bowl, sift the buckwheat flour, baking powder, nutmeg, and cinnamon together with the gluten-free baking flour. After that, whisk in the pecans that will go into the batter.
- Eggs, almond milk, ghee, vanilla extract, and pumpkin puree should all be mixed well in a separate basin. Once mixed, add this mixture to the bowl containing the dry ingredients.
- The batter should be added to the muffin pan.
- Combine the remaining pecans, sunflower seeds, pepitas, shredded coconut, and cinnamon to make your topping. Sprinkle the topping over the batter for the muffins and softly push it down to keep it in place.
- When inserting a toothpick, bake for 20 to 25 minutes, or until it is clean. Before removing them from the muffin tin, give them some time to cool.
- With a dollop of coconut yogurt, serve right away or store it in the fridge for up to three days. For up to a month, freeze any leftover muffins.

NUTRITION SERVING SIZE: 1
CALORIES:219 FAT:16g CHOLESTEROL:53mg CARBOHYDRATES: 16g
FIBER: 3g SUGAR: 2g PROTEIN: 4g

Chocolate Chia Pudding

PREP TIME: 15 MINS. ADDITIONAL TIME: 3 HOURS. Serves 4
INGREDIENTS
PANTRY
- ☐ 1 3/4 cup Almond milk
- ☐ 1/2 cup Chia seeds
- ☐ 1/4 cup Cacao powder
- ☐ 1/2 tsp Ground Ceylon cinnamon
- ☐ 1/2 tsp Vanilla extract
- ☐ 1/8 tsp Salt

FRUIT
- ☐ 2 Dates (pits removed)

INSTRUCTIONS
- Place all the ingredients in a bowl, except the dates. To blend, whisk well.
- For 3 to 5 hours, or until the mixture resembles pudding, cover and chill the mixture.

- Blend until smooth and creamy after adding to a blender along with the dates.
- accompanied with some fruit, almonds, and coconut whipped cream and served cold.

NUTRITION SERVING SIZE: 1
CALORIES:182 FAT:9g CARBOHYDRATES:21g FIBER:10g SUGAR: 5g PROTEIN: 6g

Slow-Cooked Brownies

PREP TIME: 30 MINS COOK TIME: 2 HOURS 30 MINS Serves 16
INGREDIENTS
PROTEIN
- ☐ 3 Eggs (whisked)

PANTRY
- ☐ 1/4 cup Coconut oil
- ☐ 1/3 cup Rice malt syrup
- ☐ 1/4 cup Coconut flour
- ☐ 2 tbsp Cacao powder
- ☐ 1/2 tsp Vanilla extract
- ☐ 1/4 tsp Baking powder
- ☐ 1/4 tsp Ground Ceylon cinnamon
- ☐ 1.8 oz Dark chocolate
- ☐ (85% cacao) (chopped)

VEGETABLES
☐ 7.1 oz Sweet potato/yam (cooked, skin removed, and pureed)

INSTRUCTIONS
- Your slow cooker should be lined with baking paper that is greased inside and extends approximately halfway up the sides.
- In a bowl, combine all the dry ingredients.
- The eggs, coconut oil, rice malt syrup, and sweet potato puree should all be combined in a separate dish.
- Mix everything well after adding the dry components to the wet ones.
- Spread it evenly within the slow cooker after pouring.
- Cook for two hours on low or one hour on high.
- A skewer inserted into the middle should come out clean after another 30 minutes of cooking after removing the cover.

NUTRITION SERVING SIZE: 1
CALORIES: 104 FAT: 6g CARBOHYDRATES: 11g FIBER: 1g SUGAR: 4g PROTEIN: 2g

Snacks

Trail Mix

PREP TIME: 10 MINS
COOK TIME: 15 MINS Servings 12
INGREDIENTS
- ☐ 1 cup Cashew nuts
- ☐ 1 cup Pecans
- ☐ 1 cup Almonds
- ☐ 1 1/2 cup Coconut flakes
- ☐ 1 tbsp Stevia/Monkfruit erythritol blend
- ☐ 1/2 tsp Ground Ceylon cinnamon
- ☐ 1/2 tsp Salt
- ☐ 1 tbsp Coconut oil (melted)
- ☐ 100g Chocolate bar (85%-90% cacao) (chopped)

INSTRUCTIONS
- Put parchment paper on a baking pan and preheat the oven to 325°F (165°C).

- Combine all the ingredients in a bowl, except the chocolate, and season with salt to taste. Spread on the baking sheet after mixing.
- 15 minutes of baking time with one midway stirring.
- After removing the meal from the oven, let it cool.
- Stir in the chopped chocolate after adding it.
- For up to four weeks, keep in an airtight container in a cold, dry location.

NUTRITION SERVING SIZE: 1
CALORIES:298 FAT:24g CHOLESTEROL:2mg CARBOHYDRATES: 19g FIBER: 4g SUGAR: 10g PROTEIN: 6g

Guacamole

PREP TIME: 5 MINS.   Serves 4
PANTRY
- ☐ Salt to taste
- ☐ Pepper to taste

VEGETABLES
- ☐ 1 Tomato (finely diced)
- ☐ 1/2 Onion (finely diced)
- ☐ 1/2 cup Fresh cilantro/coriander

FRUIT
- ☐ 3 Avocados (pit removed)
- ☐ 2 tbsp Lime juice

INSTRUCTIONS
- With a fork, mash the avocado flesh after scooping it into a bowl.
- Season with salt and pepper to taste and mix in the remaining ingredients.
- If you won't be serving it right away, cover it with plastic wrap and put it in the refrigerator.
- Press the plastic wrap firmly on top of the dip so that it doesn't come into touch with air to prevent the guacamole from browning.

NUTRITION INFORMATION: YIELD: 4 SERVING SIZE: 1
CALORIES:256 FAT:22g CARBOHYDRATES:16g FIBER:11g SUGAR: 3g PROTEIN: 4g

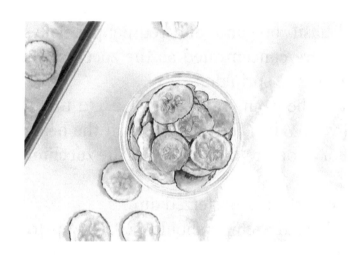

Zucchini Chips

PREP TIME: 10 MINS COOK TIME: 2 HOURS 30 MINS SERVINGS: 2

Ingredients
Pantry
- ☐ 1 tbsp Olive oil
- ☐ 1 tsp Salt

Vegetable
- ☐ 2 Zucchinis

INSTRUCTIONS

- Two baking sheets should be lined with parchment paper and the oven should be preheated to 200°F (100°C). For this recipe, use parchment paper if possible since it will assist the chips to get crispy on the bottom.
- Slice the zucchini very thinly, to a thickness of 1/16" to 1/8" (1.5 to 3 mm). If you have a mandolin slicer, this task is simple, but with patience and care, you can also do it with a sharp knife.
- Olive oil should be drizzled over the zucchini in a bowl before being gently mixed to coat.
- On the baking sheets, arrange the disks tightly together (but not touching). Add salt to taste along with any other spices you'd want to test. While basic salted zucchini chips are fantastic, additional tasty minglings include cumin, coriander, and chili powder; smoked paprika; and basil, oregano, and red pepper flakes. Since the spices will become more concentrated as the zucchini shrinks in the oven, you only need a little sprinkle.
- Put the dish in the oven, and bake for 2 1/2 to 3 hours, or until it is crisp and brown. When finished, turn off the heat and hold the oven door open. For another 30 minutes, let the zucchini cool in the heated oven.
- Enjoy alone or with your preferred dip.
- In a zip-top bag, the chips should last for up to 3 days, although during this period, they could soften. But I don't think you'll have any issues going through them.

NUTRITION INFORMATION: YIELD: 2 SERVING SIZE: 1
Amount Per Serving: CALORIES: 90 TOTAL FAT: 7g CHOLESTEROL: 0mg SODIUM: 1169mg CARBOHYDRATES: 5g FIBER: 2g SUGAR: 3g PROTEIN: 2g

SMOOTHIES

Supercharged Green Smoothie

PREP TIME: 10 MINS. Serves 2
INGREDIENTS
PANTRY
- ☐ 2.5 cup Almond milk
  (or unsweetened flax milk)

VEGETABLES
- ☐ 1 cup Kale
  (de-stemmed and chopped)
- ☐ 1 cup Rainbow chard (chopped)
- ☐ 1 cup Baby spinach
- ☐ 1/2 Carrot (chopped)

FRUIT
- ☐ 1/2 Avocado
- ☐ 1/2 Apple (cored and chopped)
- ☐ 1/2 cup Frozen blueberries

INSTRUCTIONS
- Blend the leafy greens and half the amount of almond milk in a blender. until smooth, process.
- Process once more after adding the additional ingredients.
- Maintains quality when refrigerated for two days.

NUTRITION SERVING SIZE: 1
CALORIES: 237 FAT: 11g CARBOHYDRATES: 34g FIBER: 10g SUGAR: 10g PROTEIN: 6g

Nutty Chai Smoothie

PREP TIME: 5 MINS   Serving 2
INGREDIENTS
PANTRY
- ☐ 1 1/2 cup Almond milk (or coconut milk)
- ☐ 1 cup Cashew nuts (soaked in water overnight, drained)
- ☐ 2 tbsp Coconut butter

- ☐ 1 tsp Vanilla extract
- ☐ 1 tsp Ground Ceylon cinnamon
- ☐ 1 tsp Ground cardamom
- ☐ 1/2 tsp Ginger powder
- ☐ 1/16 tsp Salt

FRUIT
- ☐ 1/2 Banana (frozen)

OTHER
- ☐ 1 cup Ice

INSTRUCTIONS
- The ingredients should be thoroughly smooth after being combined in a blender.
- Pour the mixture into a serving glass, top with some more cinnamon, and serve.

NUTRITION SERVING SIZE: 1
CALORIES: 580 FAT:44g CARBOHYDRATES:41g FIBER:7g SUGAR: 14g PROTEIN: 13g

Spicy Veggie Smoothie

PREP TIME: 5 MINs Servings 2
INGREDIENTS
PANTRY
- ☐ 1 cup Coconut water

- ☐ 1/2 tsp Cayenne powder

VEGETABLES
- ☐ 1 cup Baby spinach
- ☐ 1 Tomato (roughly chopped)
- ☐ 1 Carrot (roughly chopped, frozen)
- ☐ 1 Cucumber (roughly chopped, frozen)
- ☐ 1 tsp Garlic (minced)

FRUIT
- ☐ 1 Avocado (fresh or frozen)
- ☐ 1 Lime (peeled)

INSTRUCTIONS

- Add a pinch of salt after blending all the ingredients in a high-speed blender. Include the lime juice as well as its meat. until smooth, process.
- Pour into two glasses for serving, then sip.

NUTRITION SERVING SIZE: 1

CALORIES: 235 FAT:15g CARBOHYDRATES:26g FIBER:11g SUGAR: 9g PROTEIN: 5g

21 DAY MEAL PLAN

Week 1:
Breakfast:
Day 1: Oatmeal With Berries And Nuts
Day 2: Sausage McMuffin
Day 3: Spicy Chicken Breakfast Bake
Day 4: Pumpkin Pancakes
Day 5: TEX-MEX Breakfast Skillet
Day 6: Granola Bake
Day 7: Breakfast Blues Porridge

Lunch:
Day 1: Salad With Grilled Chicken or Fish
Day 2: Soup
Day 3: Carrot, Orange and Avocado Salad
Day 4: Panzanella Salad
Day 5: Sandwich on whole-wheat bread with lean protein and vegetables
Day 6: Tuna salad sandwich
Day 7: Chicken Salad Sandwich

Dinner:
Day 1: Pulled Pork
Day 2: Creamy Tomato Baked Fish
Day 3: Zambreros Burrito Bowl
Day 4: Harvest Chicken Chili
Day 5: Shrimp Fried Rice
Day 6: Zuppa Toscana
Day 7: Slow Cooked Beef and Broccoli

Snacks:
Trail Mix
Guacamole
Zucchini chips
Smoothie

Week 2:
Breakfast:
Day 8: Yogurt parfait
Day 9: Overnight oats
Day 10: Egg muffins
Day 11: Breakfast burrito
Day 12: Breakfast Sandwich
Day 13: Oatmeal With Berries And Nuts
Day 14: Sausage MacGuffin

Lunch:
Day 8: Quinoa bowl with black beans, corn, and salsa
Day 9: Tofu stir-fry
Day 10: Veggie wrap
Day 11: Salad with chickpeas
Day 12: Soup
Day 13: Carrot, Orange and Avocado Salad
Day 14: Panzanella Salad

Dinner:
Day 8: Creamy Tomato Baked Fish
Day 9: Zambreros Burrito Bowl
Day 10: Harvest Chicken Chili
Day 11: Shrimp Fried Rice
Day 12: Zuppa Toscana
Day 13: Slow Cooked Beef and Broccoli
Day 14: Pulled Pork

Snacks:
Trail Mix
Guacamole
Zucchini chips
Smoothie

Week 3:
Breakfast:
Day 15: Tomato and Watermelon Salad
Day 16: Smoothie with protein powder
Day 17: Greek yogurt with fruit and granola
Day 18: Whole-wheat toast with avocado
Day 19: Hard-boiled eggs
Day 20: Oatmeal With Berries And Nuts
Day 21: Sausage McMuffin

Lunch:
Day 15: Sandwich on whole-wheat bread with lean protein and vegetables
Day 16: Tuna salad sandwich
Day 17: Chicken Salad Sandwich
Day 18: Salad With Grilled Chicken or Fish
Day 19: Soup
Day 20: Carrot, Orange and Avocado Salad
Day 21: Panzanella Salad

Dinner:
Day 15: Creamy Tomato Baked Fish
Day 16: Zambreros Burrito Bowl
Day 17: Harvest Chicken Chili
Day 18: Shrimp Fried Rice
Day 19: Zuppa Toscana
Day 20: Slow Cooked Beef and Broccoli
Day 21: Pulled Pork

Snacks:
Trail Mix
Guacamole
Zucchini chips
Smoothie

Made in United States
Troutdale, OR
08/20/2023